COLLECTED LATER POEMS

THE COMPLETE TEXTS OF

THE TRANSPARENT MAN

FLIGHT AMONG THE TOMBS

THE DARKNESS AND THE LIGHT

COLLECTED
LATER
POEMS

ANTHONY
HECHT

Alfred A. Knopf   *New York*   2003

Library of Congress Cataloging-in-Publication Data
Hecht, Anthony, [date]
[Poems. Selections]
Collected later poems / by Anthony Hecht.—1st ed.
p.   cm.
Contains three previously published collections: The transparent man,
Flight among the tombs, and The darkness and the light.
ISBN 1-4000-4138-4
I. Title.
PS3558.E28A6 2003
811'.54—dc21
2003044601

For Helen

Oh my most dear, I know the live imprint
        Of that smile of gratitude,
Know it more perfectly than any book.
        It brims upon the world, a mood
Of love, a mode of gladness without stint.
O that I may be worthy of that look.

CONTENTS

THE TRANSPARENT MAN

I

II

III

IV

V

FLIGHT AMONG THE TOMBS

I THE PRESUMPTIONS OF DEATH

II PROUST ON SKATES

THE DARKNESS AND THE LIGHT

THE TRANSPARENT MAN

For HELEN and for EVAN

I

CURRICULUM VITAE

As though it were reluctant to be day,
    Morning deploys a scale
    Of rarities in gray,
And winter settles down in its chain-mail,

Victorious over legions of gold and red.
    The smokey souls of stones,
    Blunt pencillings of lead,
Pare down the world to glintless monotones

Of graveyard weather, vapors of a fen
    We reckon through our pores.
    Save for the garbage men,
Our children are the first ones out of doors.

Book-bagged and padded out, at mouth and nose
    They manufacture ghosts,
    George Washington's and Poe's,
Banquo's, the Union and Confederate hosts',

And are themselves the ghosts, file cabinet gray,
    Of some departed us,
    Signing our lives away
On ferned and parslied windows of a bus.

RIDDLES

And the Spirit of God moved upon
the face of the waters.

Where the wind listeth, there the sailboats list,
     Water is touched with a light case of hives
Or wandering gooseflesh. The strange power and gist
     Of whatever it is that animates our lives

Scrawls with a lavish hand its signature
     Of ripples gathered into folds and pleats
As indecipherable, chiselled, pure,
     And everlasting as the name of Keats.

The surface wrinkles in spirit-shapes that sprint
     Like small rapids or frightened schools of fish;
They blot out images of cloud, the print
     Of passing hulls, obeying something's wish.

These vagrant hieroglyphs, now here, now there,
     In which the fate of everything lies writ
By the invisible majesty of air,
     Prove we are one and all illiterate,

And should be asking: "What do they portend?"
     Other, please God, than those fiery words for coins
That signified to Belshazzar the end
     Of all his hopes and the issue of his loins.

CHORUS FROM *OEDIPUS AT COLONOS*

What is unwisdom but the lusting after
Longevity: to be old and full of days!
For the vast and unremitting tide of years
Casts up to view more sorrowful things than joyful;
And as for pleasures, once beyond our prime,
They all drift out of reach, they are washed away.
And the same gaunt bailiff calls upon us all,
Summoning into Darkness, to those wards
Where is no music, dance, or marriage hymn
That soothes or gladdens. To the tenements of Death.

Not to be born is, past all yearning, best.
And second best is, having seen the light,
To return at once to deep oblivion.
When youth has gone, and the baseless dreams of
    youth,
What misery does not then jostle man's elbow,
Join him as a companion, share his bread?
Betrayal, envy, calumny and bloodshed
Move in on him, and finally Old Age—
Infirm, despised Old Age—joins in his ruin,
The crowning taunt of his indignities.

So is it with that man, not just with me.
He seems like a frail jetty facing North
Whose pilings the waves batter from all quarters;
From where the sun comes up, from where it sets,
From freezing boreal regions, from below,
A whole winter of miseries now assails him,
Thrashes his sides and breaks over his head.

TERMS

For Derek Walcott

Holidays, books and lives draw to their close,
The curtain rings down on some theater piece,
The brass, string, and percussion sections close
In on their tonic and concordant close
When all loose ends infallibly are tied
Into baroque or plain completion. Close
Your eyes, and a childhood landscape wades in close
With delicate birch to supplant the frank disgrace
Of our littoral, littered world, as painters grace
A woman's grief, a beggar's bowl, with close
Clear scrutiny until a world has grown
Out of Rembrandt's pain and a narrow ghetto's groan.

Open your eyes. A body of water has grown
Obsidian, slick and ballroom smooth. Look close,
And, through a wind's light pucker, mark full-grown
Migrations of clouds, to which small fish have grown
Accustomed, which they inhabit, all of a piece
With their rock-bottom skies. And now the grown
Wind-wrinkles, the mackerel heavens, with their
    ingrown
Pisces and constellated summertide
Calm for an instant, arresting the whole tide
Of time, like ants in amber, momently grown
Changeless and still as painting, fluttering grace
Notes that are held in mind by an act of grace.

The young are full of an astonishing grace,
Soft-eyed, trustful and lithe till they have grown
Aware of being admired for their grace,
Whereupon they go through some fall from grace,
An aging that reminds us of our close.
The skater's tilt, the contemplator's grace

Are both a selflessness, evincing grace
In agile tension as well as mastered peace,
In a poise of speed or stillness. But our last peace,
Stone-capped, dark-rooted, engraved and void of grace,
Beds down in rain and rubble, and eventide
Sees us unsinewed, our last lank strands untied.

What do those distant thunderheads betide?
Nothing to do with us. Not our disgrace
That the raped corpse of a fourteen-year-old, tied
With friction tape, is found in a ditch, and a tide
Of violent crime breaks out. Yet the world grown
Wrathful, corrupt, once loosed a true floodtide
That inched inside the wards where the frail are tied
To their beds, invaded attics, climbed to disclose
Sharks in the nurseries, eels on the floors, to close
Over lives and cries and herds, and on that tide,
Which splintered barn, cottage and city piece-
Meal, one sole family rode the world to peace.

Think of the glittering morning when God's peace
Flooded the heavens as it withdrew the tide:
Sweet grasses, endless fields of such rich peace
That for long after, when men dreamed of peace,
It seemed a place where beast and human grace
A pastoral landscape, a Virgilian peace,
Or scene such as Mantegna's masterpiece
Of kneeling shepherds. But that dream has grown
Threadbare, improbable, and our paupers groan
While "stockpiled warheads guarantee our peace,"
And troops, red-handed, muscle in for the close.
Ours is a wound that bleeds and will not close.

Long since we had been cautioned: "Until he close
His eyes forever, mildly and in peace,
Call no man happy." The stain of our disgrace
Grows ominously, a malign, ingrown
Melanoma, softly spreading its dark tide.

DEVOTIONS OF A PAINTER

Cool sinuosities, waved banners of light,
Unfurl, remesh, and round upon themselves
In a continuing turmoil of benign
Cross-purposes, effortlessly as fish,
On the dark underside of the foot-bridge,
Cast upward against pewter-weathered planks.
Weeds flatten with the current. Dragonflies
Poise like blue needles, steady in mid-air,
For some decisive, swift inoculation.
The world repeats itself in ragged swatches
Among the lily-pads, but understated,
When observed from this selected vantage point,
A human height above the water-level,
As the shore shelves heavily over its reflection,
Its timid, leaf-strewn comment on itself.
It's midday in midsummer. Pitiless heat.
Not so much air in motion as to flutter
The frail, bright onion tissue of a poppy.
I am an elderly man in a straw hat
Who has set himself the task of praising God
For all this welter by setting out my paints
And getting as much truth as can be managed
Onto a small flat canvas. Constable
Claimed he had never seen anything ugly,
And would have known each crushed jewel in the
     pigments
Of these oily golds and greens, enamelled browns
That recall the glittering eyes and backs of frogs.
The sun dispenses its immense loose change,
Squandered on blossoms, ripples, mud, wet stones.

I am enamored of the pale chalk dust
Of the moth's wing, and the dark moldering gold
Of rust, the corrupted treasures of this world.
Against the Gospel let my brush declare:
"These are the anaglyphs and gleams of love."

DESTINATIONS

The harvest is past, the summer is
ended, and we are not saved. JEREMIAH

The children having grown up and moved away,
One day she announced in brisk and scathing terms
That since for lo, as she said, these many years
She had thanklessly worked her fingers to the bone,
Always put him and the children first and foremost,
(A point he thought perhaps disputable)
She had had it up to here, and would be leaving
The following day, would send him an address
To which her belongings could be forwarded
And to which the monthly payments could be sent.
He could see her point. It was only tit for tat.
After all the years when the monthly pains were hers
They now were to be his. True to her word,
Which she commanded him to mark, she packed
And left, and took up shifting residence,
First with a barber, then with a state trooper:
From the scissors of severance to the leather holster
Of the well-slung groin—the six-pack, six-gun weapon
Of death and generation. He could see the point.
In these years of inflation ways and means
Had become meaner and more chancy ways
Of getting along. Economy itself
Urged perfect strangers to bed down together
Simply to make ends meet, and so ends met.
Rather to his surprise, his first reaction
Was a keen sense of relief and liberation.
It seemed that, thinking of her, he could recall
Only a catalogue of pettiness,
Selfishness, spite, a niggling litany
Of minor acrimony, punctuated
By outbursts of hysteria and violence.
Now there was peace, the balm of Gilead,
At least at first. Slowly it dawned upon him
That she had no incentive to remarry,

Since, by remaining single and shacking up,
She would enjoy two sources of income.
In the house of her deferred and mortgaged dreams
Two lived as cheaply as one, if both had funds.
He thought about this off and on for years
As he went on subsidizing her betrayal
In meek obedience to the court decree,
And watered the flowers by his chain-link fence
Beside the railroad tracks. In his back yard
He kept petunias in a wooden tub
Inside the white-washed tire of a tractor trailer,
And his kitchen steps of loose, unpainted boards
Afforded him an unimpeded view
Of the webbed laundry lines of all his neighbors,
Rusted petroleum tins, the buckled wheels
Of abandoned baby-carriages, and the black-
Sooted I-beams and girders of a bridge
Between two walls of rusticated stonework
Through which the six-fifteen conveyed the lucky
And favored to superior destinies.
Where did they go, these fortunates? He'd seen
Blonde, leggy girls pouting invitingly
In low-cut blouses on TV commercials,
And thought about encountering such a one
In a drugstore or supermarket. She
Would smile (according to his dream scenario)
And come straight home with him as if by instinct.
But in the end, he knew, this would be foreplay
To the main event when she'd take him to the cleaners.

ECLOGUE OF THE SHEPHERD AND THE TOWNIE

SHEPHERD

Not the blue-fountained Florida hotel,
Bell-capped, bellevued, straight-jacketed and decked
With chromium palms and a fromage of moon,
Not goodnight chocolates, nor the soothing slide
Of huîtres and sentinel straight-up martinis,
Neither the yacht heraldic nor the stretch
Limos and pants, Swiss banks or Alpine stocks
Shall solace you, or quiet the long pain
Of cold ancestral disinheritance,
Severing your friendly commerce with the beasts,
Gone, lapsed, and cancelled, rendered obsolete
As the gonfalon of Bessarabia,
The shawm, the jitney, the equestrian order,
The dark daguerreotypes of Paradise.

TOWNIE

No humble folding cot, no steaming sty
Or sheep-dipped meadow now shall dignify
Your brute and sordid commerce with the beasts,
Scotch your flea-bitten bitterness or down
The voice that keeps repeating, "Up your *Ars
Poetica,* your earliest diapered dream
Of the long-gone Odd Fellows amity
Of bunny and scorpion, the *entente cordiale*
Of lamb and lion, the old nursery fraud
And droll Aesopic zoo in which the chatter
Of chimp and chaffinch, manticore and mouse,
Diverts us from all thought of entrecôtes,
Prime ribs and rashers, filets mignonnettes,
Provided for the paired pythons and jackals,

Off to their catered second honeymoons
On Noah's forty-day excursion cruise."

SHEPHERD

Call it, if this should please you, but a dream,
A bald, long-standing lie and mockery,
Yet it deserves better than your contempt.
Think also of that interstellar darkness,
Silence and desolation from which the Tempter,
Like a space capsule exiled into orbit,
Looks down on our green cabinet of peace,
A place classless and weaponless, without
Envy or fossil fuel or architecture.
Think of him as at dawn he views a snail
Traveling with blind caution up the spine
Of a frond asway with its little inching weight
In windless nods that deepen with assent
Till the ambler at last comes back to earth,
Leaving his route, as on the boughs of heaven,
Traced with a silver scrawl. The morning mist
Haunts all about that action till the sun
Makes of it a small glory, and the dew
Holds the whole scale of rainbow, the accord
Of stars and waters, luminously viewed
At the same time by water-walking spiders
That dimple a surface with their passages.
In the lewd Viennese catalogue of dreams
It's one of the few to speak of without shame.

TOWNIE

It is the dream of a shepherd king or child,
And is without all blemish except one:

That it supposes all virtue to stem
From pure simplicity. But many cures
Of body and of spirit are the fruit
Of cultivated thought. Kindness itself
Depends on what we call consideration.
Your fear of corruption is a fear of thought,
Therefore you would be thoughtless. Think again.
Consider the perfect hexagrams of snow,
Those broadcast emblems of divinity,
That prove in their unduplicable shapes
Insights of Thales and Pythagoras.
If you must dream, dream of the ratio
Of Nine to Six to Four Palladio used
To shape those rooms and chapels where the soul
Imagines itself blessed, and finds its peace
Even in chambers of the *Malcontenta,*
Those just proportions we hypostatize
Not as flat prairies but the City of God.

MEDITATION

For William Alfred

> *Quatrocento put in paint,*
> *On backgrounds for a God or Saint,*
> *Gardens where the soul's at ease;*
> *Where everything that meets the eye*
> *Flowers and grass and cloudless sky*
> *Resemble forms that are, or seem*
> *When sleepers wake and yet still dream,*
> *And when it's vanished still declare,*
> *With only bed and bedstead there,*
> *That Heavens had opened.*

I

The orchestra tunes up, each instrument
In lunatic monologue putting on its airs,
Oblivious, haughty, full of self-regard.
The flute fingers its priceless strand of pearls,
Nasal disdain is eructed by the horn,
The strings let drop thin overtones of malice,
Inchoate, like the dense garbling of voices
At a cocktail party, which the ear sorts out
By alert exclusions, keen selectivities.
A five-way conversation, at its start
Smooth and intelligible as a Brahms quintet,
Disintegrates after one's third martini
To dull orchestral nonsense, the jumbled fragments
Of domestic friction in a foreign tongue,
Accompanied by a private sense of panic:
This surely must be how old age arrives,
Quite unannounced, when suddenly one fine day
Some trusted faculty has gone forever.

II

After the closing of cathedral doors,
After the last soft footfall fades away,
There still remain artesian, grottoed sounds
Below the threshold of the audible,
The infinite, unspent reverberations
Of the prayers, coughs, whispers and *amens* of the day,
Afloat upon the marble surfaces.
They continue forever. Nothing is ever lost.
So the sounds of children, enriched, magnified,
Cross-fertilized by the contours of a tunnel,
Promote their little statures for a moment
Of resonance to authority and notice,
A fleeting, bold celebrity that rounds
In perfect circles to attentive shores,
Returning now in still enlarging arcs
To which there is no end. Whirled without end.

III

This perfect company is here engaged
In what is called a sacred conversation.
A seat has been provided for the lady
With her undiapered child in a bright loggia
Floored with *antico verde* and alabaster
Which are cool and pleasing to the feet of saints
Who stand at either side. It is eight o'clock
On a sunny April morning, and there is much here
Worthy of observation. First of all,
No one in all the group seems to be speaking.
The Baptist, in a rude garment of hides,
Vaguely unkempt, is looking straight at the viewer
With serious interest, patient and unblinking.

Across from him, relaxed but powerful,
Stands St. Sebastian, who is neither a ruse
To get a young male nude with classic torso
Into an obviously religious painting,
Nor one who suffers his target martyrdom
Languidly or with a masochist's satisfaction.
He experiences a kind of acupuncture
That in its blessedness has set him free
To attend to everything except himself.
Jerome and Francis, the one in his red hat,
The other tonsured, both of them utterly silent,
Cast their eyes downward as in deep reflection.
Perched on a marble dais below the lady
A small seraphic consort of viols and lutes
Prepares to play or actually is playing.
They exhibit furrowed, child-like concentration.
A landscape of extraordinary beauty
Leads out behind the personages to where
A shepherd tends his flock. Far off a ship
Sets sail for the world of commerce. Travelers
Kneel at a wayside shrine near a stone wall.
Game-birds or song-birds strut or take the air
In gliding vectors among cypress spires
By contoured vineyards or groves of olive trees.
A belfry crowns a little knoll behind which
The world recedes into a cobalt blue
Horizon of remote, fine mountain peaks.

   The company, though they have turned their backs
To all of this, are aware of everything.
Beneath their words, but audible, the silver
Liquidities of stream and song-bird fall
In cleansing passages, and the water-wheel
Turns out its measured, periodic creak.

They hear the coughs, the raised voices of children
Joyful in the dark tunnel, everything.
Observe with care their tranquil pensiveness.
They hear all the petitions, all the cries
Reverberating over marble floors,
Floating above still water in dark wells.
All the world's woes, all the world's woven woes,
The warp of ages, they hear and understand,
To which is added a final bitterness:
That their own torments, deaths, renunciations,
Made in the name of love, have served as warrant,
Serve to this very morning as fresh warrant
For the infliction of new atrocities.
All this they know. Nothing is ever lost.
It is the condition of their blessedness
To hear and recall the recurrent cries of pain
And parse them into a discourse that consorts
In strange agreement with the viols and lutes,
Which, with the water and the meadow bells,
And every gathered voice, every *amen*,
Join to compose the sacred conversation.

II

SEE NAPLES AND DIE

*It is better to say, "I'm suffering," than
to say, "This landscape is ugly."* SIMONE WEIL

I

I can at last consider those events
Almost without emotion, a circumstance
That for many years I'd scarcely have believed.
We forget much, of course, and, along with facts,
Our strong emotions, of pleasure and of pain,
Fade into stark insensibility.
For which, perhaps, it need be said, thank God.
So I can read from my journal of that time
As if it were written by a total stranger.
Here is a sunny day in April, the air
Cool as spring water to breathe, but the sun warm.
We are seated under a trellised roof of vines,
Light-laced and freaked with grape-leaf silhouettes
That romp and buck across the tablecloth,
Flicker and slide on the white porcelain.
The air is scented with fresh rosemary,
Boxwood and lemon and a light perfume
From fields of wild-flowers far beyond our sight.
The cheap knives blind us. In the poet's words,
It is almost time for lunch. And the *padrone*
Invites us into blackness the more pronounced
For the brilliance of out-doors. Slowly our eyes
Make out his pyramids of delicacies—
The Celtic coils and curves of primrose shrimp,
A speckled gleam of opalescent squid,
The mussel's pearl-blue niches, as unearthly
As Brazilian butterflies, and the grey turbot,
Like a Picasso lady with both eyes
On one side of her face. We are invited
To choose our fare from this august display
Which serves as menu, and we return once more
To the sunshine, to the fritillary light

And shadow of our table where carafes
Of citrine wine glow with unstable gems,
Prison the sun like genie in their holds,
Enshrine their luminous spirits.
                                    There, before us,
The greatest amphitheater in the world:
Naples and its Bay. We have begun
Our holiday, Martha and I, in rustic splendor.
I look at her with love (was it with love?)
As a breeze takes casual liberties with her hair,
And set it down that evening in the hotel
(Where I make my journal entries after dinner)
That everything we saw this afternoon
After our splendid lunch with its noble view—
The jets of water, Diana in porphyry,
Callipygian, broad-bottomed Venus,
Whole groves of lemons, the packed grenadine pearls
Of pomegranate seeds, olive trees, urns,
All fired and flood-lit by this southern sun—
Bespoke an unassailable happiness.
And so it was. Or so I thought it was.
I believe that on that height I was truly happy,
Though I know less and less as time goes on
About what happiness is, unless it's what
Folk-wisdom celebrates as ignorance.
Dante says that the worst of all torments
Is to remember happiness once it's passed.
I am too numb to know whether he's right.

II

Over the froth-white cowls of our morning coffee
I read to Martha from a battered guide-book
Which quotes a seventeenth-century diarist,

Candid and down-to-earth, on Naples' whores.
The city, he declared, proudly maintained
A corps of thirty-thousand registered sinners,
Taxed and inspected, issued licenses
For the custom of their bodies. One may assume
Their number, and the revenues of the state,
Must have compounded since those early days.
There were accounts, as well, of female beggars
With doped and rented children, and a rich trade
In pathos by assorted mendicants.
Baedeker, who is knowing in these matters,
Warns travelers against misguided kindness:
The importunate should be rebuffed with *niente*,
He firmly advises, and goes on to say
That poverty is a feature of the landscape.
Perhaps this strong fiduciary theme
Prompted attention to our own resources.
A six- or seven-year-old good-looking urchin
Had posted himself each day across the street
From our hotel, and from this vantage point
He offered tourists good black-market rates
Of currency exchange. I fell for this
For what, I suppose, are all the usual reasons.
There was first of all the charming oddity
Of a child-financier plying his trade
With such bright confidence. There was my pride,
The standard, anxious pride of every tourist,
Of wishing to exhibit worldly cunning
And not be subject to official rates.
And there was finally the curious lure
Of doing something questionably legal,
Which I could have no chance to do at home.
So I let the boy guide me through dark back alleys
To a small, grim, unprepossessing square,

Festooned with drying sheets and undergarments
Strung like blank banners high above our heads,
The ensigns of our nameless, furtive business.
He motioned me to wait, and disappeared.
There were two men across the square from me,
Conspicuous, vaguely thuggish, badly dressed,
In lively discourse, paying me no notice,
But filling me with a mild apprehension.
I could hear the whines of children, the louder wails
Of ambulances on their urgent missions
Somewhere far off, claiming their right of way.
The area smelled of garlic, soap, and urine.
And then young Ercole made his appearance.
He introduced himself. He was short, dark,
Athletic, with an air of insolence.
He was neatly dressed with very expensive shoes
In which he evidently took some pride,
A complex wrist-watch boasting several dials,
And delicate hands decked with a dazzle of rings.
Pride, as it seems, was governing us both.
I felt distinctly uncertain of myself
But saw no way before me to withdraw.
I noticed that as our talk got underway
The men across the square had ceased conversing
And were giving us their full consideration,
Which, given the cautious nature of our dealings,
Was far from reassuring. But Ercole,
Who seemed aware that we were being watched,
Was undismayed, and so I went along.
We came to terms. I had my travelers' checks,
And he had bills of large denominations
Rolled into wads, stuffed in his jacket pockets.
He mockingly let me examine one.
It seemed genuine enough. I agreed to exchange

Two hundred dollars' worth of travelers' checks.
He counted out the bills before my eyes,
Folded them neatly into a thick packet,
And I in turn carefully signed my checks,
And we made our exchange. And then he smiled
A smile of condescension and insolence,
Waved to me with a well-manicured hand
On which he wore a number of gold rings
And disappeared. Throughout this both of us
Knew we had been intensively observed
By the two thugs who stood across the square.
They must have seen the large bulge in my pocket
And I was now certainly too mistrustful
To count the bills once more in sight of them
Or ask of them the way to my hotel.
So I made the return home by trial and error,
And only within the confines of my room
Did I discover that my wad of bills
Was almost wholly folded newspaper.
At first, of course, I was furious; Martha thought me
A gullible fool, which didn't improve my mood.
Two hundred dollars is not a trifling sum,
But after a while I began to realize
That Ercole's fine clothes were the pathetic
Costume and *bella figura* of the poor.
For him, like other Neapolitan sinners,
Staying alive, the sheer act of survival,
Was a game of cunning I was quite unused to
And involved paying off confederates:
The helpless urchin outside our hotel,
The two thuggish observers, whose mere presence
Had kept me from discovering the fraud
Until too late, and may have distracted me
(I pride myself on being a keen observer)

From the skilled legerdemain of those adept,
Tapered, manicured, bejewelled hands.

III

See, what a perfect day. It's perhaps three
In the afternoon, if one may judge by the light.
Windless and tranquil, with enough small clouds
To seem like innocent, grazing flocks of heaven.
The air is bright with a thickness of its own,
Enveloping the cool and perfect land,
Where earthly flocks wander and graze at peace
And men converse at ease beside a road
Leading to towers, to battlements and hills,
As a farmer guides his cattle through a maze
Of the chipped and broken headstones of the dead.
All this, serene and lovely as it is,
Serves as mere background to Bellini's painting
Of *The Transfiguration*. Five dazzled apostles,
Three as if just awakening from sleep,
Surround a Christ whose eyes seem to be fixed
On something just behind and above our heads,
Invisible unless we turned, and then
The mystery would indeed still be behind us.
A rear-view mirror might perhaps reveal
Something we cannot see, outside the picture
But yet implied by all Bellini's art.
Whatever it is seems to be understood
By the two erect apostles, one being Peter,
The other possibly John, both of them holding
Fragments of scroll with Hebrew lettering,
Which they appear just to have been consulting.
Their lowered eyes indicate that, unseeing,
They have seen everything, have understood

The entire course of human history,
The meaning and the burden of the lives
Of Samson, Jonah, and Melchizedek,
Isaiah's and Zechariah's prophecies,
The ordinance of destiny, the flow
And tide of providential purposes.
All hope, all life, all effort has assembled
And taken human shape in the one figure
There in the midst of them this afternoon.
And what event could be more luminous?
His birth had been at night, and at his death
The skies would darken, graves give up their dead.
But here, between, was a day so glorious
As to explain and even justify
All human misery and suffering.
Or so, at least, perhaps, the artist felt,
And so we feel, gazing upon a world
From which all pain has cleanly been expunged
By a pastoral hand, moving in synchronous
Obedience to a clear and pastoral eye.
        By this time, having gazed upon as much
Painting in the *Museo Nazionale*
As could reasonably be taken in
On a single morning, we make our way outside
Only to be confronted by the *pompe*
Funebri of six jet-black harnessed chargers,
Each with black ostrich plumes upon his head,
Drawing a carriage-hearse, also beplumed,
Black but glass-walled, and bearing a black coffin
Piled with disorderly hot-house profusions
Of lilies, gladioli, and carnations.
The sidewalk throngs all cross themselves, and Martha
Seems especially and mysteriously upset
In ways I fail to understand until

Back in our room she breaks out angrily:
"Didn't you see how small the coffin was?"
I am bewildered by this accusation.
Of course I *saw*, but thought it far more prudent
To leave the topic delicately untouched.
I am annoyed at her and at myself,
An irritation I must not let damage
What yet remains of this holiday of ours.

IV

Two days of rain. Confining. Maddening.
From our French windows and our small *balcon*
We watch the cold, unchanging, snake-skinned bay
Curtained by leaden sheets of rain in which
Capri and Procida are set adrift
Beyond the limits of sight, like the *Wandering Isles*.
We are housebound, quarantined. We read and fret,
Trying our best to be cheerful and good humored,
And it occurs to me that only a nation
Devoted to the cult of the Madonna
With all its doctrinal embellishments
Could produce "extra-virgin olive oil."
Martha is not amused by this; the rain
Has damped her spirits, and she has been reading
Grand-guignol sections on Tiberius
In Suetonius' gossipy old book.
The weather itself feels like those steel engravings
Of the *Inferno* by Gustave Doré:
A ruthless, colorless, unvarying gray.
So that when sunshine comes we are astonished,
Filled with both gratitude and with amazement
At the brilliant flowers in the public squares.
We elect to spend the morning simply sunning

In the great park of the *Villa Nazionale*,
And find ourselves almost restored to normal
When we become reluctant witnesses
To a straggling parade of freaks and mutants
From a local hospital for the handicapped
On a brief outing to the aquarium.
They are extraordinary: stunted, maimed,
Thalidomide deformities, small, fingerless,
Mild pigmentless albinos, shepherded
Into a squeaky file by earnest nuns
Between the sunlit bushes of azaleas.
They seem like raw material for the painting
Of Bosch's *Temptation of St. Anthony:*
Wild creatures, partly human, but with claws
Or camel humps, or shrivelled, meager heads.
What they will see inside those glassy tanks
(Thick sullen eels, pale sea-anemones)
Will be no odder than what they are themselves.
Martha, who never ventures anywhere
Without me, and has not a word of Italian,
Has disappeared.
               I am deeply alarmed.
It suddenly seemed that she might be the victim
Of some barbaric or unthinkable crime:
That, kidnapped, she was being held for ransom,
Or worse. I hurried back to the hotel,
And found her, deeply shaken, in our room,
Unwilling to talk, unwilling, at first, to listen
To any attempt to soothe or comfort her.
I tried to tell her in what must have been
A way that somehow frightened or offended
That life required us to steel ourselves
To the all-too-sad calamities of others,
The brute, inexplicable inequities,

To form for ourselves a carapace of sorts,
A self-preservative petrific toughness.
At this she raised her arm, shielding her eyes
As if she thought I were about to strike her,
And said *No* several times, not as a statement,
But rather as a groan. And then she gave me
A look the like of which I can't describe.
I left her in possession of the room
And spent the rest of the day pacing the lobby,
Taking my tea alone. She finally joined me
For a dinner at which not a word was uttered
On either side.
               What struck me during the meal
(As if confirming everything I'd told her)
Was a vivid recollection from that morning:
Not of the warped and crippled, but of the reds,
Among the pale profusions of azaleas,
The brilliant reds of the geraniums.

V

Somewhere along in here, deeply depressed,
I ceased making journal entries, so what follows
Is pretty much an uncertain reconstruction
Concerning our brief excursion to the baths
Of Nero and the surrounding countryside.
It was intended as a light diversion
Into the realms of luxury and ease,
A little apolaustic interval.
Were we wrong, I wonder, to expect so much?
I looked at the map, and saw the *Mare Morto*,
And innocently thought of the Holy Land.
We entrusted ourselves meekly to the hands
Of a guide (found for us by our concierge),

An older man of dignified appearance
Who spoke fair English and was named Raimondo.
His smile was reassuring; we were both
Impressed and pleased by his enthusiasm.
Baiae was once a fashionable resort.
Caesar and Nero and Caligula
Had built their summer villas on this coast.
But Nero's baths were desultory ruins,
Tangled in chicory and acanthus growth,
Littered by tourists, and excrement of dogs.
The hills around are honey-combed with caves,
And Raimondo told us with naive excitement
Of the Sibyl's Cave, the old worldly-wise Sibyl
Who cunningly foxed and outwitted Tarquin,
Obliging him to buy her three last books
For the full price of nine by coolly burning
A set of volumes each time he refused.
But first Raimondo had another cave
Picked for our delectation: damp and foul-smelling,
It was, of course, the well-known *Grotta del Cane,*
Known in the ancient texts as *Charon's Cave.*
The brimstone odors here rise from a depth
No one can measure, keeping the very earth
Throughout this region perpetually warm—
So much that when Raimondo cut some turf
With a penknife and handed me a clod
I could feel heat from subterranean fires.
It's to these bottomless thermal wells of warmth
That all this region owes its opulence,
Its endless summer *wo die Zitronen blühn.*
A man and a mongrel now enter the cave,
Answering Raimondo's summons. We are to view
The ghastly and traditional death-scene.
But only after the no less traditional

And ceremonious haggling about fees,
A routine out of *commedia dell'arte.*
And then, by the scruff of the neck, the master forces
His dog's head close to a rank and steaming fissure
Where fumes rise from the earth, the stink of Dis,
That place of perfect hospitality
"Whose ancient door stands open night and day."
The dog's eyes widen in unseeing terror;
It yelps feebly, goes into wild convulsions,
And then falls limp with every semblance of
Death. Being then removed and laid
Near the cave's mouth, in about thirty seconds
It starts to twitch and drool, then shakes itself,
And presently staggers to its four feet.
With a broad wink and conspiratorial smile,
Raimondo says that by modest computation
That dog dies three hundred times a year,
And has been earning its own livelihood
As well as its owner's for about three years.
This puts it well ahead of Lazarus,
Orpheus, and the others who have made
Sensational returns. As the Sibyl said
Solemnly to Aeneas, "The way down
Is easy from Avernus—but getting back
Requires a certain amount of toil and trouble."
Avernus, as it happens, the stinking lake
No bird can fly across, all birds avoid,
Lies within easy access, as does the Cave
Of Cumaean Sibyl, both of which Raimondo
Encourages us to visit, but we insist
That we have had enough of caves and smells
To last us for a while, so he proposes
A little tour of the Elysian Fields,
The region of the blurred and blissful dead.

Virgil had made it seem a lovely place,
A heroes' health-club, a gymnasium
Of track-stars, wrestlers, athletes, all engaged
In friendly contest, sun-tanned rivalry.
Here, too, convened all those distinguished ghosts
Who had bettered life by finding out new truths,
Inventing melodies or making verses,
At home in a faultless landscape of green meadows
Watered by streams of dazzling clarity.
What we saw was something different. There was, of
    course,
No fabulous descent to a nether world.
Instead Raimondo took us to a place
Where, we assumed, he meant to let us pause
Before some planned approach to the sublime.
But he said to us, quite lamely, "This is it.
This is the place called the Elysian Fields."
(I checked his claim that evening in the guide-book,
And the map proved that he had told the truth.)
It was a vacant wilderness of weeds,
Thistles and mulberries, with here and there
Poplars, quite shadeless; thick, ramshackle patches
Of thorny amaranth, tousled by vines.
This wild, ungoverned growth, this worthless, thick,
And unsuppressible fecundity
Was dotted with a scattering of graves
Of the most modest sort: worn, simple stones
From which all carving had been long effaced,
And under which the mute, anonymous dead
Slept in supreme indifference to the green
Havoc about them, the discourse of guides,
The bewildered tourists, acres of desolation.

VI

Marriages come to grief in many ways.
Our own was, I suppose, a common one,
Without dramatics, a slow stiffening
Of all the little signs of tenderness,
Significant silences, self-conscious efforts
To be civil even when we were alone.
The cause may be too deep ever to find,
And I have long since ceased all inquiry.
It seems to me in fact that Martha and I
Were somehow victims of a nameless blight
And dark interior illness. We were both
Decent and well-intentioned, capable
Of love and devotion and all the rest of it,
Had it not been for what in other ages
Might have been thought of as the wrath of God,
The cold, envenoming spirit of Despair,
Turning what was the nectar of the world
To ashes in our mouths. We were the cursed
To whom it seemed no joy was possible,
The spiritually warped and handicapped.
It seems, in retrospect, as I look over
The pages of this journal, that the moments
Of what had once seemed love were an illusion,
The agreement, upon instinct, of two people
Grandly to overestimate each other,
An accord essentially self-flattering,
The paradise of fools before the fall.
What sticks in the mind, what I cannot escape,
Is the setting in which we found ourselves that day
I first began to see us as outcast:
The ugliness of the landscape, the conviction
That no painter would think it worth a glance.

There are both places and periods in life
That are tolerable only as transitions;
Hell might consist in staying there forever,
Immobile, never able to depart.
Such was the vision I received that day,
Raised, as it chanced, to perhaps the ultimate power
By reading the letters of the Younger Pliny.
His distinguished uncle, the revered old man,
Author of the great *Natural History*
In thirty-seven volumes, was stationed here
On this promontory, just where I had been,
At the time disaster struck. There had been flames
And leaping fires made the more terrible
By the darkness of the night. He was a stout man,
And, from the fumes and smoke, found it hard to
    breathe.
But he had tied a pillow over his head
As protection against falling rocks and pumice,
And calmly went about to satisfy
His scientific curiosity.
Of all those strange sights the most ominous
Was perhaps the sudden vision of the sea
Sucked out and drained away by the earthquake
That was part of the eruption, leaving a sea-bed
Of naked horrors lighted now and then
By jets of fire and sheet-lightning flares,
Only to be folded back into the dark.
One could make out in such brief intervals
An endless beach littered with squirming fish,
With kelp and timbers strewn on muddy flats,
Giant sea-worms bright with a glittering slime,
Crabs limping in their rheumatoid pavane.

III

A LOVE FOR FOUR VOICES

Homage to Franz Joseph Haydn

For Frank and Ruth Glazer

FIRST VIOLIN	HERMIA
SECOND VIOLIN	HELENA
VIOLA	LYSANDER
CELLO	DEMETRIUS

I   *Allegro Moderato*

HERMIA

Here we have fallen transposingly in love,
And the fireflies, the Japanese lanterns, flare
With little conjugate passions, images of
The cordial, chambered ignitions of the heart.
Far down below, the lilting, debonair
Pleasure craft blink and wander in the cove
Like slippery constellations, as if man's art
Had made a prayer rug of the firmament,
A broad-loomed duplicate night wherein to trace
Patterns of happy prospect, drawn from the blent,
Breath-taking features of a cherished face.

Lemon verbena blooms in the tufa wall,
And the mild night air, warm as our whispered words,
Circulates like a bloodstream, invisible
Yet parallel as smooth ascending thirds
To our most inward workings. Warmth and youth,
All the clear promptings of this clement weather,
Invest our bodies with a looming truth
To be pursued and husbanded together.

LYSANDER

Playing along the fringe of this delight
    Slides a strange warning finger,
Not hers, not mine, not the blind god of love's
    (To whom we serve as braille)
But yet indicative of another night
    Prepared as though with cloves
In the fixed future, where neither glance shall linger
    Nor pulse nor god prevail.

Diminished sevenths, modular descents
    Full of alarming jumps
And sudden accidentals strike a note,
    Brief as a lovers' quarrel,
That shakes us with an obscure significance.
    Like a whiff of creosote
Tainting the garden, they proclaim in trumps
    The *carpe noctem* moral.

These dissonances but serve to underscore
    The score nobody knows
Except the taciturn composer, Fate.
    Sensing at the deep base
Of our being the ultimate cadences before
    They gather to their close,
We feel the fickle fingering and confess
    It's already getting late.

HELENA

You think you know who you are, when all at once
      You stand amazed:
Love has pulled off one of its major stunts,
And the routine view in the mirror now displays
Merits unrecognized in other days.
      The weather's clear and fine,
Or, if it's raining, everything is glazed,
      Becrystalled and benign.

But who's that nymph the cheval glass now discloses?
      This calls for thought.
It seems to you you've seen her. Couched on roses?
Attended by a little, wingèd brood?
Somewhere. Perhaps in Kenneth Clark's "The Nude,"
      Bearing the alias
Of *Miss O'Murphy*, or superbly wrought
      In ravishing undress

By Renoir or Correggio or Lachaise.
      All this is due
To the interest and the steady, upright ways
Of a lad who seems the third, or efficient, cause
Of a sort of constant ringing of applause
      Or oceanic roar
Mounting in acclamations just for you
      From the whole Atlantic shore.

And then you know: you are the latest find
      Of Hollywood
Featured in private screenings of the mind

In an inventory of post-Freudian sex
Called "Civilization and its Discothèques."
    In a lingua franca phrase
Of body language at last you've understood
    What gauds and gilds your days.

DEMETRIUS

Mine is the firm bass clef that shall unlock
A world of passions in our *théâtre à clef*
Which is all about the ways of human clay
When freed from the simple props of summer stock.

Enter, Myself, for a turn about the stage.
I muse on the causes of my ecstasy,
Displayed well-stacked in billowing deshabille,
Yielding in levantine concubinage.

Yet I am nothing if not cynical.
Wherein does she delight me save in this:
That I indorse upon her with a kiss
A mound attaining to some pinnacle,

That there's no feature of me but promotes
Her insatiety, that I adore
Merely my lonely self as, more and more,
I am the singular thing on which she dotes.

I am Narcissus, she simply the pool,
Obliging, selfless, bright, wherein I see
Intoxicating images of Me,
Classical, isolate, withdrawn and cool.

TUTTI

Now, in a highly sharpened signature,
We sign away our lives for the duration,
And each of us, determined on seduction,
Makes his insinuating overture.
Organ involuntaries, crotchet songs,
Bed chamber measures, operatic lays,
Each goes its cunning, predetermined ways,
Seeking the counterpart for which it longs.

Time's of the essence, and will not permit
Eight hands, eight legs, two staffs and one joint purpose
Any returning, any starting over,
Nor can the ingenuities of wit
Alter the text or term of this our opus
That binds in ligatures beloved and lover.

II   *Minuetto: Presto ma non troppo*

LYSANDER

Question: Isn't to fall in love to fall
Away from Time or out of it, to break
Tempo in a sort of contretemps,
Flouting the linear ways of chronicle?
Only in fantasies and tales of love
Can we imagine the "terminally well."

HELENA

Agreed, my dear. Love is in fact the nostrum,
Compounded of plain meum/tuum simples,
That takes its crabbed critic by the throat
And renders him a tender Juvenal.

HERMIA

Lovers and tourists enjoy the luxury
Of being set apart from daily life.
Morning refinishes Saint Polycarp
With aureate platings, sunny encrustations,
And beneath a café awning the tourist savors
Chicory-coffee fumes as a profligate fountain
Casts up before his eyes whole velvet trays
Of cabochons and brilliants. Yet what absorbs him
Are the small transformations, the differences
That invest the simplest fixtures of the world.
Windows and telephones, coins and umbrellas,
Are all, as it were, recast in foreign terms.

DEMETRIUS

And so it is, as you were going to say,
With lovers. They pass through familiar sordors,
Worn curbstones foul with uncollected garbage,
Which they translate into the Côte d'Azur.
Noting the gleam on the lip of a coffee mug,
They remember all the ricochets of light
That return from darkened corners in Vermeer,
Reflective, upon a beautiful young servant.

TUTTI

Love comes like capers to the Aurelian Wall,
Capricious, goat-like, ready to undermine
The whole imperial enterprise, and split
With little wedging tentacles and roots
The masonry of the Tabularium.
Spring and the goddess prompt these penetrations
And intimate subversions. They revive
Grape hyacinth and crocus and raise up
Daily with promise long-standing hopes and members.
Anadyomene, restless, of the waters,
Powerful, rash and salty, hear our prayer.
Make glad our passage with your ritornello;
Furnish each humble thing that greets our sight
With pure ipseity; transpose the world
With augmentations of your major theme.

III   *Andante: post coitum triste*

DEMETRIUS

Late afternoon. The canted light
Sieves down through elevated glooms
Of linden, sycamore and beech
As lengthening shadows stripe the grass.
The cricket concertmaster's A
Is taken up through the dense fields,
Heavy with scent and irony,
Dotted with common everlasting,
Bitter dock and cocklebur.
From the cool shadows of this rock,
These crowding blues and heliotropes,
As from some attic of my youth
I gaze out at the distances
That contrast renders almost white,
Like frocks of garden-party girls
I once knew or desired to know,
Speckled and flecked by shadow-leaves
Like missing jigsaw puzzle parts.
And whether the girls were known or not,
Whether those yearnings were stillborn
Or were met with kindness, now they lie
Like quilts of sunlight spread to dry,
Scattered and thin and dimly gold
And permanently out of reach—
Small flags of failure, or, at best,
Triumphs with all their glory lost.
Between post oak and propter oak
Falls the inevitable shade.

HERMIA

Out of the cotton batting clouds, the scentless gauze
     Of sleep, out of the pendulous rockabye
Of dreamt treetops, one floats down leaf-like to be
       received
     Without resistance by the sustaining bed
As, one by one, the faculties grab their discarded
     Clothing and make themselves decent, the five
Little senses answer the rollcall roster of school
     And that ten o'clock scholar, the mind, late
As always, shows up confused, asking, "Where am I?"
     Nothing's familiar. The chiffonière, majestic
In seasoned tones of briar, the tall, lead-weighted drapes
     Declare that overnight and all unmerited
You have risen in the world. And curiosity
     On just that point calls you to the window seat
At what you suppose to be the bedlington gray of pre-
       dawn.
     It's not. A long drizzle has brought the worms
To their flagstone deaths, and across the barbered lawn a
       soaked
     Flag hangs limp on its epicene pole. Neither breeze
Nor birdsong, but the drainpipe from the gutters
       overhead
     Rattles its tinny chimes or liquid vocables.
Near at hand stone urns of the balustrade darken with
       charcoal
     Weathering, and far away the trees take umbrage
In the disconsolations of the mist. And then it all comes
       back.
     You turn as if for confirmation, and there it lies,

Fred Trismegistus himself, sleeping the Sleep of the Just
    Plumb Tuckered Out, rapt in some dream of
        which he
Is the much-cheered, totally adored hero of stadiums
    Full of nubile, half-clad girls, in which he
Is the sole male, the halfback, half-baked, sexy medalist
    Who lolls in insolent Iotacism,
Giving himself up gratefully to that famous first
    Infirmity of an ignoble mind. About
Two, perhaps, he may so much come to himself as to
    Discover that what he really needs is a
Bath and a shave. But meanwhile your own clothes,
        strewn here and
    There, begin to recall your imbecilities
Of last night. What will your hostess, a friend since
        grade school, say?
    Better get dressed as quietly as possible
And slip out for a cold, long, sobering walk.

HELENA

Take Waller's stoic, gladiatorial rose,
Saluting you as it prepares to die
On orders, simply to make a vulgar point:
That Time and the poet's nose are out of joint,
That flesh is grass, and he's a blade who grows
Green till he has what you can best supply.

But for pure instruction nothing can compare
With those gigantic, momentary blooms
In the sequined colors of a two-bit whore:
Metallic-blue chrysanthemums that soar
Over our heads and homes, dangle in air,
Decline and blacken to their instant dooms

Quicker than you can say "Jack Robinson."
The question is: what are they telling us?
If life is brief, that sex is even briefer,
Its joys like the illusions of a reefer,
Decaying from the moment they're begun
And scarcely worthy of such struggle and fuss?

LYSANDER

Man, that with the heated imagination of a poet lies down in the finest linens to caresses, must rise in due course *from the sack* in all the frosty solitude of a philosopher. "How came this spell upon me," he inquires, "that made my very flesh to stand on end? made me, who am otherwise all head, vision and mind, become mere fundament, pure Bottom, someone's ass?" It is sheer fantasy confers such powers: I vote her beautiful out of my need. Her grace is in the gland of the beholder. This is plain masturbation, thinly disguised, in which I dub her my sea-born Galatea, and she brightly replies, "Baby, you're aces." Bodies themselves in plain truth are no more shapely than potatoes; they are as pallid of flesh and take up their residence under the same brown sod. Let him who can be aroused by a potato plight his true oath and purchase wedding bands. I, divested of illusions, must now inhabit among essences.

IV *Finale: vivace assai*

HELENA

What prompts the ichor of the gods
    To race along their limbs?
Young, well-developed human bods,
    Succulent hers and hims.
Shamelessly these divine ones flirt
    With those of mortal race,
And, one may add, it doesn't hurt
    Having a comely face.

LYSANDER

In divers incarnations they,
    As bull or swain or swan,
Devote themselves to carnal play
    And wildly carry on,
And gotten up in festal guise
    Or bestial masquerade
Contrive to get themselves lengthwise
    Definitively laid.

HERMIA

No quarry can elude their quest
    Or can divert the mind
Of those who batten on a breast
    Or well-defined behind.
Theirs is a gleeful *vie de bohème*
    Unbound by moral codes
In which they work the lawless claim
    Of virgin mother-lodes.

DEMETRIUS

Like smoothly polished Phidian nudes
    Of vast and sculptured shape,
They cast themselves in attitudes
    Of statutory rape.
Vigorous their pursuit of bliss,
    Emphatic and *tout court,*
From which no earthly orifice
    Is perfectly secure.

TUTTI

And shall not humble humankind
    Aspire to godly ways,
Utter the disembodied mind
    In fleshly paraphrase?
Therefore come all ye neophytes,
    Observe the Rule of Thumb;
With ever more intense delights
    And mounting pleasures, come!

HERMIA

It has been left to me now to supply
The modest coda, close and epilogue
Of this machineless masque, beg your indulgence
For all our author's incapacities,
And crave your pardon if he has offended.
The loves we have enacted, the sweet neumes
And melodies played out in artful casts
Of baited lines and characters, were not
Mere casual rousings of the rampant id.
They exhibit a certain play, free, natural,
Yet harmonious charmingly, as if our lives,
As you would like to hope, had a design
Not to be seen here in the thick of things.
But the thick of things is not beside the point.
The gray felt daylong dusk of winter skies,
The golden, noontide braveries of midsummer,
Odors of harvest apples, the cursive lines
Of one known hand, pressed clover leaves between
The India paper leaves of Second Kings,
A voice, the expectation of a voice,
Quavers of light and semibreves of joy
Confirm the only magic of the world
Here where we fall transposingly in love.

IV

ANTHEM

These birds pursue their errands
    On curvatures of air;
Like swift and lyric gerunds
    Unfurling everywhere,
They lash the sky with ribbons,
    With wakes of wrinkled blue,
Chanting Orlando Gibbons
    And Mozart's *Non so più.*

Shall we not in all conscience
    And glittering major keys
Offer them fair responsions
    And reciprocities?
Fanfares and sound fulfillings
    Of melodies unheard:
Brave philharmonious Billings
    And airs of William Byrd.

ANTAPODOSIS

For Mona and Jarvis

I

You send us your used weather, the gray serge
Of clouds, hand-me-down rain that has picked up
Its acid comment in transit through Ohio,
Second-hand blizzards, wrinkled isobars
That thunder eastward in an aerial surf.
Stuff the Salvation Army wouldn't touch!
Soiled, threadbare, obsolete, your record lows
Low like lost herds of Angus, like bull markets
Among the shivered stocks and bonds of heaven,
The china shop of stars, come blundering in
And let us have it, and of which we plain
In plaintive plainsong and the plainest terms
That the Great Plains and Hoagy Carmichael
Provide: "You've Come a Long Way From St. Louis."

II

We send you our used daylight, mildewed dawns,
Rusted sunset finales that have seen
Better days, wasted afternoons as stale,
Flat and unprofitable as *The New York Sun,*
Drypoint editions of New England dusk,
Ghostly crepuscules straight from the photo morgue.
Shrunk by inflation, our diminished savings
Of late November light, like little hairless
Chihuahuas, seem doll-house versions of the Dog Days.
And finally, the soft night having arrived,
Scented with sweetgrass, garrulous with crickets,
The sky Columbian Blue, you lift your eyes,
And what do we hand you but "The Great White Way,"
Our name in lights, somewhat the worse for where.

HUMORESQUE

Passengers will please refrain
from flushing toilets while the train
is standing in the station. I love you.

From sewage lines, man-holes, from fitted brass
Sphincters and piston chambers, from the dark
Gastro-intestinal corridors of hell,
Deep among wheels and oily underbellies
Of *Wagon Lits* emerge these screeching ghosts,
Doomed for a certain term to walk the night,
Erupting here and there in baggy forms
That cloud, occlude and spirit away the luggage,
Facteurs and passengers from this vast barn
Of skeletal iron and grimed membranes of glass.
This pestilent congregation of vapors sings
In Pentecostal tongues, now shrill, now soft,
Mixed choral dolorosos by Satie
To the god Terminus, the living end
Of every journey, whom the Romans charmed
With gifts of blood and ashes, and who today
Comes up from under as pale S. Lazare,
Come back to tell us all, and tell us off,
And tell and tell, as the bells toll and trains
Roll slowly to their sidings, issuing ghosts.
These rise and fade into the winter air
Already gray with souls of the departed
Through which indifferent pigeons lift and bank
And flutter in the vague and failing warmth,
Which, like the curling lamias of *Gauloises,*
The shiny rigor mortis of the rails,
Blends with the exhalations of my love.

NAMING THE ANIMALS

Having commanded Adam to bestow
Names upon all the creatures, God withdrew
To empyrean palaces of blue
That warm and windless morning long ago,
And seemed to take no notice of the vexed
Look on the young man's face as he took thought
Of all the miracles the Lord had wrought,
Now to be labelled, dubbed, yclept, indexed.

Before an addled mind and puddled brow,
The feathered nation and the finny prey
Passed by; there went biped and quadruped.
Adam looked forth with bottomless dismay
Into the tragic eyes of his first cow,
And shyly ventured, "Thou shalt be called 'Fred.' "

ENVOI

A voice that seems to come from outer space,
Small, Japanese (perhaps the pilot of
One of these frisbee saucer flights that trace
Piss-elegant trajectories above

Sharp eyes and index finger landing pads),
Speaks to me only with its one-watt tweeter
(A dodderer among these dancing lads)
And firmly orders: "Take me to your reader."

My Muse. I'd know her anywhere. It's true
I'm no Bob Dylan, but I've more than one
Electric fan who likes the things I do:
Putting some English on the words I've spun

And sent careening over stands of birch
To beat the local birds at their own game
Of taking off and coasting in to perch,
Even, perhaps, in pigeon-cotes of fame.

They are my chosen envoys to the vast
Black Forests of Orion and The Bear,
Posterity's faint echo of its past,
And payload lifted into haloed air.

A BOUNTIFUL HARVEST

The Rev. Elisha Fawcett, ... a Man-
chester Evangelist, ... devoted his life
to teaching the natives of the Admi-
ralty Islands the Commandments of
God and the Laws of Cricket. Too
poor to purchase a monument to this
good man, his parishioners erected
his wooden leg upon his grave. In
that fertile clime it miraculously took
root and for many years provided a
bountiful harvest of bats.

As if mistaking a foghorn for The Last Trump,
This risen limb, come forth before its time,
Dryadic, out of a turned and varnished stump,
A Lazarus with one foot still in the grave

(To whom some shameless newsman presses his query,
"What was it like ... I mean ... *you know* ... down
    there?"
And with all the sad reserve of the truly weary,
The leaves signal their dignified "No Comment"),

This umbrageous Evangelical Christmas tree
Is festooned with a troupe of gymnasts all in gray
Instead of with globes and tinsel, a filigree
Of bats, or acrobats, hung upside-down

As if to receive a well-timed fling of wrists
Or ankles, and known as "The Flying Pipistrelli."
Their capes wrapped close about them, these aerialists
Let their blood pool in their tiny frontal lobes

And dream they are now, in the words of the secular
    Pope,
"The light *Militia* of the lower Sky,"
Attendant Sprites, cruising through stroboscope,
Slow-motion frames of inner loops and dives,

Guided by sonar wit or the saintly folly
Of those the World at large describe as "batty,"
Raising their little, high-pitched, melancholy
Squeaks in a Chapel hymn by Isaac Watts.

The Commands of God and Ordinances of Cricket
Meshed and were married in the good man's sermon
Titled, "The Straight Gate is a Sticky Wicket,"
Still quoted with approval at church picnics,

And all the parish point with ordinate praise
To the leafy witness of the life that died
And rose again in green (with some scattered grays).
That went forth, was fruitful, and multiplied.

V

CROWS IN WINTER

Here's a meeting
of morticians in our trees.
They agree in klaxon voices:
things are looking good.
The snowfields signify
a landscape of clean skulls,
Seas of Tranquility
throughout the neighborhood.

Here's a mined,
a graven wisdom,
a bituminous air.
The first cosmetic pinks
of dawn amuse them greatly.

They foresee the expansion of graveyards,
they talk real estate.
Cras, they say,
repeating a rumor
among the whitened branches.

And the wind, a voiceless thorn,
goes over the details,
making a soft promise
to take our breath away.

IN MEMORY OF DAVID KALSTONE

who died of AIDS

Lime-and-mint mayonnaise and salsa verde
Accompanied poached fish that Helen made
For you and J.M. when you came to see us
Just at the salmon season. Now a shade,

A faint blurred absence who before had been
Funny, intelligent, kindness itself,
You leave behind, beside the shock of death,
Three of the finest books upon my shelf.

"Men die from time to time," said Rosalind,
"But not," she said, "for love." A lot she knew!
From the green world of Africa the plague
Wiped out the Forest of Arden, the whole crew

Of innocents, of which, poor generous ghost,
You were among the liveliest. Your friend
Scattered upon the calm Venetian tides
Your sifted ashes so they might descend

Even to the bottom of the monstrous world
Or lap at marble steps and pass below
The little bridges, whirl and eddy through
A liquified Palazzo Barbaro.

That mirrored splendor briefly entertains
Your passing as the whole edifice trembles
Within the waters of the Grand Canal,
And writhes and twists, wrinkles and reassembles.

POEM WITHOUT ANYBODY

In memory of James Wright

Mid-ocean. Nightfall. No one. The sea spray
Is spattered upward out of a dark body
As if determined to become air, and falls,
A failure, back to its laced and slippery troughs,
Its sliding, undulant gulleys of polished black.
The winds battle each other, the ravelled air
Tumbles across cold miles of desolation,
Plunging and spilling over a punished surface.
Here are no grandeurs and no sufferings,
Neither the grim particulars of wrongs
Nor hope nor courage. Here all the doubtful postures
Of history, pride, and language fall away.
The surge continues its untiring violence,
The foam of outrage, Promethean helplessness,
Bound fast to its own mindless element.

Dear Jim, I call to you across the darkness
Where we are emptied of all our vanities,
Where none of our pleas is answered. Beyond the slosh
And wet, beyond the salt tumulous puzzle,
Beyond millions of deaths, loss and injustice,
The derelict shacks, the bare neglected farms,
May it please these muscular powers to rehearse
Your pain and whispered words, lavish their tears
On all the waste of which you are the image,
And by their own tormented energy
To be lifted out of themselves, a floating mist,
Gray, neutral, passionless, and modified,
A delicate shawl of sorrow, lingering
Into horizonless indifference,
The cold, blank rock-face of a sunless day.

TO L. E. SISSMAN, 1928–1976

Now "a spring breath of Lux across the Charles"
Salutes the freshman noses that detect
On trellises of the laboring intellect
Faint emblematic blooms of Vaughan and Quarles

Along with poisonous minerals and exhausts
Of Donne and Ford and Kissinger and Chevy.
The Yard is green, and sophomores note the heavy
Strokes on the metered tennis courts of Frost's

Athletic quatrains: this *ars* which endures
Beyond the *vita brevis* will bother heads
Of bra-less, liberated, cool co-eds
For many a spring to come, craft such as yours,

Dear friend, whose poetry of Brooklyn flats
And poker sharps broadcasts the tin pan truths
Of all our yesterdays, speaks to our youths
In praise of both Wallers, Edmund and Fats,

And will be ringing in some distant ear
When the Mod-est, last immodesty fatigues,
All Happenings have happened, the Little Leagues
Of Pop and pop-fly poets disappear

To join, with all their perishable lines,
The Edsel, Frug, beau monde of Buzzard's Gulch,
The wisdom and the wit of Raquel Welch,
"And connoisseurs of California wines."

THE TRANSPARENT MAN

I'm mighty glad to see you, Mrs. Curtis,
And thank you very kindly for this visit—
Especially now when all the others here
Are having holiday visitors, and I feel
A little conspicuous and in the way.
It's mainly because of Thanksgiving. All these mothers
And wives and husbands gaze at me soulfully
And feel they should break up their box of chocolates
For a donation, or hand me a chunk of fruitcake.
What they don't understand and never guess
Is that it's better for me without a family;
It's a great blessing. Though I mean no harm.
And as for visitors, why, I have you,
All cheerful, brisk and punctual every Sunday,
Like church, even if the aisles smell of phenol.
And you always bring even better gifts than any
On your book-trolley. Though they mean only good,
Families can become a sort of burden.
I've only got my father, and he won't come,
Poor man, because it would be too much for him.
And for me, too, so it's best the way it is.
He knows, you see, that I will predecease him,
Which is hard enough. It would take a callous man
To come and stand around and watch me failing.
(Now don't you fuss; we both know the plain facts.)
But for him it's even harder. He loved my mother.
They say she looked like me; I suppose she may have.
Or rather, as I grew older I came to look
More and more like she must one time have looked,
And so the prospect for my father now
Of losing me is like having to lose her twice.
I know he frets about me. Dr. Frazer
Tells me he phones in every single day,
Hoping that things will take a turn for the better.

But with leukemia things don't improve.
It's like a sort of blizzard in the bloodstream,
A deep, severe, unseasonable winter,
Burying everything. The white blood cells
Multiply crazily and storm around,
Out of control. The chemotherapy
Hasn't helped much, and it makes my hair fall out.
I know I look a sight, but I don't care.
I care about fewer things; I'm more selective.
It's got so I can't even bring myself
To read through any of your books these days.
It's partly weariness, and partly the fact
That I seem not to care much about the endings,
How things work out, or whether they even do.
What I do instead is sit here by this window
And look out at the trees across the way.
You wouldn't think that was much, but let me tell you,
It keeps me quite intent and occupied.
Now all the leaves are down, you can see the spare,
Delicate structures of the sycamores,
The fine articulation of the beeches.
I have sat here for days studying them,
And I have only just begun to see
What it is that they resemble. One by one,
They stand there like magnificent enlargements
Of the vascular system of the human brain.
I see them there like huge discarnate minds,
Lost in their meditative silences.
The trunks, branches and twigs compose the vessels
That feed and nourish vast immortal thoughts.
So I've assigned them names. There, near the path,
Is the great brain of Beethoven, and Kepler
Haunts the wide spaces of that mountain ash.
This view, you see, has become my Hall of Fame.

It came to me one day when I remembered
Mary Beth Finley who used to play with me
When we were girls. One year her parents gave her
A birthday toy called "The Transparent Man."
It was made of plastic, with different colored organs,
And the circulatory system all mapped out
In rivers of red and blue. She'd asked me over
And the two of us would sit and study him
Together, and do a powerful lot of giggling.
I figure he's most likely the only man
Either of us would ever get to know
Intimately, because Mary Beth became
A Sister of Mercy when she was old enough.
She must be thirty-one; she was a year
Older than I, and about four inches taller.
I used to envy both those advantages
Back in those days. Anyway, I was struck
Right from the start by the sea-weed intricacy,
The fine-haired, silken-threaded filiations
That wove, like Belgian lace, throughout the head.
But this last week it seems I have found myself
Looking beyond, or through, individual trees
At the dense, clustered woodland just behind them,
Where those great, nameless crowds patiently stand.
It's become a sort of complex, ultimate puzzle
And keeps me fascinated. My eyes are twenty-twenty,
Or used to be, but of course I can't unravel
The tousled snarl of intersecting limbs,
That mackled, cinder grayness. It's a riddle
Beyond the eye's solution. Impenetrable.
If there is order in all that anarchy
Of granite mezzotint, that wilderness,
It takes a better eye than mine to see it.
It set me on to wondering how to deal

With such a thickness of particulars,
Deal with it faithfully, you understand,
Without blurring the issue. Of course I know
That within a month the sleeving snows will come
With cold, selective emphases, with massings
And arbitrary contrasts, rendering things
Deceptively simple, thickening the twigs
To frosty veins, bestowing epaulets
And decorations on every birch and aspen.
And the eye, self-satisfied, will be misled,
Thinking the puzzle solved, supposing at last
It can look forth and comprehend the world.
That's when you have to really watch yourself.
So I hope that you won't think me plain ungrateful
For not selecting one of your fine books,
And I take it very kindly that you came
And sat here and let me rattle on this way.

THE BOOK OF YOLEK

Wir haben ein Gesetz,
Und nach dem Gesetz soll er sterben.

The dowsed coals fume and hiss after your meal
Of grilled brook trout, and you saunter off for a walk
Down the fern trail, it doesn't matter where to,
Just so you're weeks and worlds away from home,
And among midsummer hills have set up camp
In the deep bronze glories of declining day.

You remember, peacefully, an earlier day
In childhood, remember a quite specific meal:
A corn roast and bonfire in summer camp.
That summer you got lost on a Nature Walk;
More than you dared admit, you thought of home;
No one else knows where the mind wanders to.

The fifth of August, 1942.
It was morning and very hot. It was the day
They came at dawn with rifles to The Home
For Jewish Children, cutting short the meal
Of bread and soup, lining them up to walk
In close formation off to a special camp.

How often you have thought about that camp,
As though in some strange way you were driven to,
And about the children, and how they were made to
    walk,
Yolek who had bad lungs, who wasn't a day
Over five years old, commanded to leave his meal
And shamble between armed guards to his long home.

We're approaching August again. It will drive home
The regulation torments of that camp
Yolek was sent to, his small, unfinished meal,
The electric fences, the numeral tattoo,
The quite extraordinary heat of the day
They all were forced to take that terrible walk.

Whether on a silent, solitary walk
Or among crowds, far off or safe at home,
You will remember, helplessly, that day,
And the smell of smoke, and the loudspeakers of the
    camp.
Wherever you are, Yolek will be there, too.
His unuttered name will interrupt your meal.

Prepare to receive him in your home some day.
Though they killed him in the camp they sent him to,
He will walk in as you're sitting down to a meal.

MURMUR

Look in thy heart and write. SIDNEY
O heart, O troubled heart— YEATS

A little sibilance, as of dry leaves,
Or dim, sibylline whisper, not quite heard:
Thus famously the powers that be converse
Just out of earshot, and theirs is the last word.
Officiously they mutter about our lives.
The die is cast, they say. *For better or worse.*

Thus the Joint Chiefs. Thus, too, the Underground.
Soft susurrations reach us where we repose
On a porch at evening. We notice a vague uproar
Of bees in the hollyhocks. Does the darkening rose
Hum with an almost imperceptible sound?
That small vibrato, is it news of a distant war?

You've seen the night nurse, who hugs your fever chart
Defensively to her bosom's alpine slopes,
Confer with an intern who lounges against a wall,
A boy not half your age. They converse apart.
And nothing they say seems to provoke a smile
As they stand there earnestly trifling with your hopes.

And remember again the long-distance telephone
When you're asked to hold the line, and way far off
A woman's cracked-voiced, broken-hearted plea
Is answered only by a toneless cough.
You have stumbled upon some gross fatality
There in the void—quite possibly your own.

This latest leak from an invisible source
Speaks like the slave appointed to hover near

The emperor, triumph-crowned in gold and myrtle,
And regularly to breathe in Caesar's ear
As they pursue the *via sacra*'s course
Through the great crowds, "Remember you are
    mortal."

FLIGHT AMONG THE TOMBS

For HELEN and EVAN

Let Mattithiah bless with the Bat,
who inhabiteth the desolations of pride
and flieth amongst the tombs.

CHRISTOPHER SMART

I THE PRESUMPTIONS OF DEATH

WOODCUTS BY LEONARD BASKIN

DEATH SAUNTERING ABOUT

The crowds have gathered here by the paddock gates
And racing silks like the flags of foreign states
     Billow and snap in the sun,
And thoroughbreds prance and paw the turf, the race
Is hotly contested, for win and show and place,
     Before it has yet begun.

The ladies' gowns in corals and mauves and reds,
Like fluently-changing variegated beds
     Of a wild informal garden,
Float hither and yon where gentlemen advance
Questions of form, the inscrutable ways of chance,
     As edges of shadow harden.

Among these holiday throngs, a passer-by,
Mute, unremarked, insouciant, saunter I,
     One who has placed—
Despite the tumult, the pounding of hooves, the sweat,
And the urgent importance of everybody's bet—
     No premium on haste.

DEATH THE HYPOCRITE

You claim to loathe me, yet everything you prize
Brings you within the reach of my embrace.
I see right through you though I have no eyes;
You fail to know me even face to face.

Your kiss, your car, cocktail and cigarette,
Your lecheries in fancy and in fact,
Unkindnesses you manage to forget,
Are ritual prologue to the final act

And certain curtain call. Nickels and dimes
Are but the cold coin of a realm that's mine.
I'm the acute accountant of your crimes
As of your real estate. Bristlecone pine,

Whose close-ringed chronicles mock your regimen
Of jogging, vitamins, and your strange desire
To disregard your assigned three-score and ten,
Yields to my absolute instrument of fire.

You know me, friend, as Faustus, Baudelaire,
Boredom, Self-Hatred, and, still more, Self-Love.
Hypocrite lecteur, mon semblable, mon frère,
Acknowledge me. I fit you like a glove.

DEATH DEMURE

I am retiring in more ways than one,
Quiet and noncommittal, a wallflower.
Reserving comment for some later hour,
I shall speak only "when all's said and done."

I hover secretly in the nightshade's
Nectar and dark, preparing my critique
Of life and manners. It's my turn to speak
When the last trump is played, in and with spades.

The softness of my voice inspires high hopes,
Weaving its way through alien environs,
Lovely as the cantatas of the Sirens
That made Odysseus heave against his ropes.

The original sheet-music of those *Femmes
Fatales* is mine, its vocal line expressive of
Sorrow? Frustration? A hopeless thirst for love?
"Nobody knows how dry (and shy) I am."

PEEKABOO
THREE SONGS FOR THE NURSERY

The longer thou livest, the more fool thou.

I

Go hide! Go hide! But through the latticework
    Of my upraised bone hands
I see athlete and statesman, priest and clerk
    Step forth as deodands,

Risking more than they know of life and limb
    In playing Peekaboo—
Whose happiest chances couldn't be called "slim"—
    I've tagged each: ICU

II

Cry, baby, cry!
You've got two reasons why.
The first is being born at all;
The second, my peremptory call.
Cry, baby, cry!

Weep, baby, weep!
No solaces in sleep.
Nightmare will ruin your repose
And daylight resurrect your woes.
Weep, baby, weep!

III

Bah, bah, black sheep, you supply the needs
Plaguing mourners: stylish widows' weeds,
Haute couture for all the fashion shows.
Black is the color of my true love's clothes.

ALL OUT

This is the way we play our little game:
While I count up to ten, the others hide.
Do what you will, it always ends the same.

Some make a classical physique their aim
And, courting lust or envy, they decide
That is the way we play our little game.

Some seek the fragile garnitures of fame,
While some drop out, claiming, to salve their pride,
"Do what you will, it always ends the same."

Others attempt to put the world to shame,
Rejoicing when their flesh is mortified.
This is the way we play our little game

Of penance and contrition, meant to tame
A fear that we shall yet be caught and tried.
Do what you will, it always ends the same,

As careful studies of the odds proclaim,
And, although universally denied,
This *is* the way we play our little game.
Do what you will, it always ends the same.

DEATH RIDING INTO TOWN

Here comes Clint Eastwood riding into town,
    One of the horsey Four
Of the Apocalypse, who won renown
    With Famine, Plague and War.

Note the official badge he seems to flaunt,
    His casual offhand grace,
Ponder his polished six-guns and his gaunt
    Uncommonly pale face.

Dürer observed him pass at an easy trot,
    Accompanied by the Devil;
To some a hero by whom the human lot
    Is finally bulldozed level.

Exalted manna is his name and sweet
    To all the long suffering,
Who kneel to embrace him, clasping his bone feet,
    His scythe, ashes and sting,

While to the light of heart and proud of purse
    Encountered on his way
He smiles his cryptic smile and bids a terse
    "Go ahead, make my day!"

DEATH THE INQUISITOR

My testimonies are wonderful to the ears of the wise;
    They shall not be gainsaid by the ignorant.
Who has searched more deeply,
    Or reached a more perfect understanding?
I have ministered to the needs of maggots
    And confabulated with the least of ants.
In the tenements of the worm, in the mansions of the
       spider
    I have kept my counsel and watched.
I have conversed with the skulls of jackals
    And interpreted the long silences.
Observing the slow accretions of coral,
    I have rejoiced in perfect peace.
Who shall number the generations of the microbe,
    Or the engenderings of the common bacillus?
Who has attended the pathologies of the whelk,
    Or measured the breathing of the lungfish?
I abide the corruption of tungsten,
    The decay of massed granite.
I shall press to the core of every secret.
    There is no match for my patience.

DEATH THE OXFORD DON

Sole heir to a distinguished laureate,
I serve as guardian to his grand estate,
And grudgingly admit the unwashed herds
To the ten-point mausoleum of his words.
Acquiring over years the appetite
And feeding habits of a parasite,
I live off the cold corpus of fine print,
Habited with black robes and heart of flint,
The word made flesh for me and me alone.
I gnaw and gnaw the satisfactory bone.

DEATH AS A MEMBER OF
THE HAARLEM GUILD OF ST. LUKE

Not just another Hals, all starch and ruff—
Some boorish member of the bourgeoisie—
I am an artisan; take note of me:
Cabinetmaker, *intarsiatori* buff,
With a honed scalpel delicate enough
To limn foreshortened lutes, books, masonry
In pearwood, sandalwood and ebony,
As a marquetry still life, a *trompe l'oeil* bluff.
And yet my clients, scorning expertise,
As if my carving hand were called in doubt,
Venture capriciously to do without
Even lapped, fished, or mitered joints, decline
My chiseled skills, discountenance my fees
And settle for a simple box of pine.

DEATH THE KNIGHT

I am my lady's champion, a knight *sans peur*,
Though bitterly reproached by everyone.
She is the world's night nurse and *paix du coeur*,
Faithful and chaste as a dark-habited nun.

When in my armor I am coldly dressed,
My noble lady's favor you may see
Boldly displayed upon my helmet's crest.
Defer to her: *La Belle Dame Sans Merci.*

DEATH THE ARCHBISHOP

... and the almond tree shall flourish, and the grasshopper shall be a burden, and desire shall fail; because man goeth to his long home; and the mourners go about the streets.

Ah my poor erring flock,
Truant and slow to come unto my ways,
    Making an airy mock
Of those choice pastures where my chosen graze,
You loiter childishly in pleasure's maze,
    Unheedful of the clock.

Mere tuneless vanities
Deflect you from the music of my word;
    You haste or take your ease
As if your cadences could be deferred,
Giving your whole consent to brief, absurd
    And piping symphonies.

The crozier, alb and cope
Compose the ancient blazons of my truth
    Whose broad intent and scope
Shows how discordant are the glees of youth,
How weak the serum of that serpent's tooth
    The ignorant call *Hope.*

Yet shall you come to see
In articles and emblems of my faith
    That in mortality
Lies all our comfort, as the preacher saith,
And to the blessèd kingdom of the wraith
    I have been given the key.

DEATH THE SOCIETY LADY

Now get you to my lady's chamber, and tell
her, let her paint an inch thick, to this
favor she must come; let her laugh at that.

Money, my dear, is my Demosthenes,
Gilead's balm, Lord God of maître d's,
Granting, like innocence, untroubled sleep,
While ugliness is no more than skin-deep.

DEATH THE POET
A BALLADE-LAMENT FOR THE MAKERS

Where have they gone, the lordly makers,
Torchlight and fire-folk of our skies,
Those grand authorial earthshakers
Who brought such gladness to the eyes
Of the knowing and unworldly-wise
In damasked language long ago?
Call them and nobody replies.
Et nunc in pulvere dormio.

The softly-spoken verbal Quakers
Who made no fuss and told no lies;
Baroque and intricate risk-takers,
Full of elliptical surprise
From Mother Goose to Paradise
Lost and Regained, where did they go?
This living hand indites, and dies,
Et nunc in pulvere dormio.

Old Masters, thunderous as the breakers
Tennyson's eloquence defies,
Beneath uncultivated acres
Our great original, Shakespeare, lies
With Grub Street hacks he would despise,
Quelled by the common ratio
That cuts all scribblers down to size,
Et nunc in pulvere dormio.

Archduke of Darkness, who supplies
The deadline governing joy and woe,
Here I put off my flesh disguise
Et nunc in pulvere dormio.

DEATH THE PAINTER

Snub-nosed, bone-fingered, deft with engraving tools,
    I have alone been given
The powers of Joshua, who stayed the sun
    In its traverse of heaven.
Here in this Gotham of unnumbered fools
I have sought out and arrested everyone.

Under my watchful eye all human creatures
    Convert to a *still life*,
As with unique precision I apply
    White lead and palette knife.
A model student of remodelled features,
The final barber, the last beautician, I.

You lordlings, what is Man, his blood and vitals,
    When all is said and done?
A poor forked animal, a nest of flies.
    Tell us, what is this one
Once shorn of all his dignities and titles,
Divested of his testicles and eyes?

DEATH THE JUDGE

Here's Justice, blind as a bat,
(Blind, if you like, as Love)
And yet, because of that,
Supreme exemplar of

Unbiased inquiry,
Knowing ahead of time
That nobody is free
Of crime or would-be crime,

And in accordance (closed
To Fortitude, Repentance,
Compassion) has composed
His predetermined sentence,

And in his chambers sits
Below a funeral wreath
And grimaces and spits
And grins and picks his teeth.

DEATH THE MEXICAN
REVOLUTIONARY

Wines of the great châteaux
Have been uncorked for you;
Come, take this terrace chair;
Examine the menu.
The view from here is such
As cannot find a match,
For even as you dine
You're so placed as to watch
Starvation in our streets
That gives your canapé
A more exquisite taste
By contrast, like the play
Of shadow and of light.
The misery of the poor
Appears, as on TV,
Set off by the allure
And glamour of the ads.
We recommend the quail,
Which you'd do well to eat
Before your powers fail,
For I inaugurate
A brand-new social order
Six cold, decisive feet
South of the border.

DEATH THE PUNCHINELLO

KENT: *This is not altogether fool, my lord.*

FOOL: *No, faith, lords and great men will not
let me. If I had a monopoly out, they
would have part on't. And ladies too,
they will not let me have all the fool
to myself; they'll be snatching.*

Two servants were paid to set his house on fire
And, when he fled, to pierce him with little darts.
And so this man, widely praised and admired,
Envied by many, a soldier, philosopher,
A young Adonis, was dead at forty-six.
So much, alas, for Alcibiades.
Now as for me, admittedly grotesque,
Cheated of feature by dissembling Nature,

Bearing an envious mountain on my back
Where sits deformity to mock my body,
I'm your imperishable comedian.
I suffer multi-interments, executions,
Yet like Donne's lovers, I die and rise the same,
Vulgar, mean, selfish, undefeatable.
You wouldn't think me much to look at me,
A clown's hooked nose and all the rest of it,
Yet, for all that, I have a way with women.
Love 'em and leave 'em, as I like to say.
And nothing pleases the kids more than my cudgel.
They see the justice of it, don't you see.
How, against all odds, this ugly man,
Hated, unmanumitted just like them,
Wields his big stick and whacks authority
Hard on its wooden head. I lack the graces
That everyone observed in the young Greek,
Women and men alike. He grew so vain
He wouldn't play the flute, claimed it distorted
The sculptural virtues of his classic features.
That, I would venture to say, is not my problem.
You find me always dressed, made-up, in white,
All dredged in flour, like an apprentice baker,
Though sometimes masked, like your Jack Ketch, in
    black.
And you, my dears, are the butt of all my jokes.
In candor, I admit some do not like me.
They call me "Toad," and they would not be far
From the truth, if only they were speaking German.
Nevertheless, in spite of such abuse,
I have a joke that always breaks them up.
Mine's the last laugh, the terminal ha-ha.
As the poet said, *"Ce crapaud-là, c'est moi."*

DEATH THE WHORE

I

Some thin gray smoke twists up against a sky
Of German silver in the sullen dusk
From a small chimney among leafless trees.
The paths are empty, the weeds bent and dead;
Winter has taken hold. And what, my dear,
Does this remind you of? You are surprised
By the familiar manner, the easy, sure
Intimacy of my address. You wonder,
Whose curious voice is this? Why should that scene
Seem distantly familiar? Did something happen
Back in my youth on a deserted path
Late on some unremembered afternoon?
And now you'll feel at times a fretful nagging
At the back of your mind as of something almost
    grasped
But tauntingly and cunningly evasive.
It may go on for months, perhaps for years.
Think of the memory game that children played
So long ago. A grownup brought a tray
Laden with objects hidden by a shawl
Or coverlet with fine brocaded flowers
Beneath which, like the roofs of a small city,
Some secret things lay cloaked. Then at a signal
The cloth was whisked away for thirty seconds.
You were allowed to do nothing but look,
And then the cover was replaced. Remember?
The tray contained bright densely crowded objects,
Sometimes exotic—a small cloisonné egg,
A candle-snuffer with an ivory handle—
But simple things as well. It never occurred
To any of the children there to count them;
You had been told simply to memorize

The contents of the tray. Each child was given
Paper and pencil to list what he recalled
And no one ever finally got them all;
Something always escaped. Perhaps a needle,
A gum eraser or a plastic ruler.
And so it is that now, as you're about
To eat or light a cigarette, something
Passes too swiftly before you can take aim,
Passes in furtive silence, in disguise,
Glimpsed only hazily in retrospect—
Like a clock's strokes recounted once they're done,
Never with confidence.
                                          And now you're angry
At what you think of as my long digression
When in fact it's the eclipses of your mind,
Those sink-holes, culverts, cisterns long avoided
As dangerous, where the actual answer lies.
As for my indirection, I'll just say
I have more time than I know what to do with.
Let me give you a hint. The voice you hear
Is not the voice of someone you remember—
Or rather, it's that voice now greatly altered
By certain events of which you've partly heard,
Partly imagined, altogether feared.
Does that help? No, I didn't think it would.
Perhaps we can return another time
(A time when you're conveniently abstracted)
To the topic of my voice and of that smoke.

II

Much time elapses. (I could count the days;
You, for your part, have no idea how many.)
Today a color ad for undergarments,

Some glossy pages of *Victoria's Secret,*
Modeled by a young blonde catches your eye.
Nothing so vivid as a memory
Results. Perhaps a vague erotic sense,
A fleeting impulse down between your legs,
Stirs like a sleeping dog. Your mind begins
Its little, paltry Leporello's list
Of former girlfriends who pass in review
As images, stripped even of their names.
And then you linger upon one. It's me.
Don't be surprised. All that was long ago.
Your indolent thought goes over my young breasts,
Remembering, fondling, exciting you.
How very long ago that was. It lasted
Almost two years. Two mainly happy years.
In all that time, what did you learn of me?
My name, my body, how best to go about
Mutual arousal, my taste in food and drink
And what would later be called "substances."
(These days among my friends I might be called
"A woman of substance" if I were still around.)
You also learned, from a casual admission,
That I had twice attempted suicide.
Tact on both sides had left this unexplored.
We both seemed to like sex for the same reason.
It was, as they used to say, a "little death,"
A tiny interval devoid of thought
When even sensation is so localized
Only one part of the body seems alive.
And when you left I began the downhill slope.
First one-night stands; then quickly I turned pro
In order to get all the drugs I wanted.
My looks went fast. I didn't really care.
The thing that I'd been after from the first,

With you, with sex, with drugs, was oblivion.
So it was easy. A simple overdose
Knocked back with half a bottle of good Scotch.
In later years the rumors found you out
Through mutual friends. And somehow you
   remembered
That I had been disowned by my family.
My parents would have nothing to do with me
After they found I'd been a prostitute,
To say nothing of my trial suicides.
So, as you guessed, when I at last succeeded,
They acted as if I never had been born.
("Let the day perish . . . ," as the scripture says.)
There was no funeral, no cemetery,
Nowhere for you to come in pilgrimage—
Although from time to time you thought of me.
Oh yes, my dear, you thought of me; I know.
But less and less, of course, as time went on.
And then you learned by a chance word of mouth
That I had been cremated, thereby finding
More of oblivion than I'd even hoped for.
And now when I occur to you, the voice
You hear is not the voice of what I was
When young and sexy and perhaps in love,
But the weary voice shaped in your later mind
By a small sediment of fact and rumor,
A faceless voice, a voice without a body.

As for the winter scene of which I spoke—
The smoke, my dear, the smoke. I am the smoke.

DEATH THE FILM DIRECTOR

Open with a long shot. Chimneys and spires
Of the old town, rouged in the copper glow
Of sunset. Intense, arterial red
Dyeing the trees as day slowly expires,
Staining the churches, pathways, fence-posts, spread
From roof to roof, while, rising from below,
Cool tides of shadow lap the countryside,
Engulf the cemetery headstones, shroud
Arbor, toolshed, curbstone and portico.
Now from behind a lazily drifting cloud
A full, Pierrot-white moon; its bleaching light
Drains the lifeblood of everything in sight.
Zoom down to a derelict alley, a scrawny cat
Sniffing through toppled garbage till it finds
A male, black-skinned, mature, immobile hand,
Its parent limb, head, body, all concealed
By liquor cartons, broken Venetian blinds,
Worn tires, an unravelled welcome mat.
The creature paws at a finger, which remains
Inert, sniffs once again, looks up and walks
Calmly across the hand into the dark.
Credits. The title, the studio, the stars
Flash on, then fade. Henry Mancini noise.
And then my name glows on the darkened screen.
It lingers there a while, etching the mind
Of every member of the audience.
As well it should. This film required of me
Immense executive abilities—
All those subordinates to keep in line,
Trained to alert me with their signal cries:
"Ready when *you* are, C.B." That's what I like,
That fine docility. As for the cast,
If the truth be known, actors are idiots.
Theirs is the glamour, of course. Their gorgeous looks,

Along with large, unmerited salaries,
Must compensate them for their tiny minds.
But in the end, after repeated takes,
The prints, the cutting-room floor, I am the one
Who sees that everything falls into place,
The master plan. This film has a large cast,
A huge cast; countless, you might almost say;
And for them all, for every one of them,
I have designed, with supreme artfulness,
What could be called an inevitable plot.

DEATH THE COPPERPLATE PRINTER

I turn Christ's cross till it turns Catherine's wheel,
Ixion's wheel becoming Andrew's cross,
    All four being windlass ways
To press my truth full home, force you to feel
    The brevity of your days,
Your strength's, health's, teeth's, desire's and memory's
        loss.

The bitten plate, removed from its Dutch Bath
Of mordants, has been set below a screw
    That will enforce my will
Like the press that crushed Isaiah's grapes of wrath.
    My lightest touch can kill,
My costly first impressions can subdue.

Slowly I crank my winch, and the bones crack,
The skull splits open and the ribs give way.
    Who, then, thinks to endure?
Confess the artistry of my attack;
    Admire the fine gravure,
The trenched darks, the cross-hatching, the pale gray.

This is no metaphor. Margaret Clitherow,
A pious woman, even as she prayed
    Was cheated of her breath
By a court verdict that some years ago
    Ordered her pressed to death.
I'm always grateful for such human aid.

DEATH THE SCHOLAR

No opinion, however absurd or incredible,
can be imagined which has not been main-
tained by one of the philosophers. DESCARTES

I bide my time, you see, I bide my time.
Recently I resumed work on the classics.
I find among these well-patinaed relics
Some glacier-capped *aiguilles* of the sublime.

Sophocles, for example: *The best of fates . . .*
And the Elder Pliny: *The supreme happiness*
Of life is that it end abruptly. Yes,
We share these quiet, twin-skulled *tête-à-têtes.*

Come, let me be the tutor to your hopes.
My scholarly emendations can expose
All your most cherished errors. I am of those
Who may be called authentic philanthropes.

Ignorance: the one unpardonable crime.
Your Solons, Stagirites, your *philosophes*
To me are countrified, unpolished oafs.
I bide my time, you see, I bide my time.

DEATH THE CARNIVAL BARKER

con brio

Step forward, please! Make room for those in back!
Come in and see the greatest show on earth!
I promise it will take your breath away!
Something you're sure to call your money's worth;
And bound to last forever and a day!
Softer than down; more powerful than crack!

Flame-eaters, jugglers, the two-headed boy
Are merely trifles by comparison.
We've got the ultimate show to freak you out.
The surest cure for worry under the sun—
As well as toothache, blindness, debt and gout.
There's nothing that you'll ever more enjoy!

The little lady with the long blonde hair
Will issue you a ticket for the price
Of your life savings, your miserable estate,
The shirt right off your back. Take my advice:
It's the best deal you'll ever get. Why wait?
We're known throughout the world as fair and square.

And talk of fairness! Talk of equality!
Give me your poor, your homeless. I admit
The halt, the deaf, all races and all trades.
O you rejected ones, unwashed, unfit,
Entrust yourselves to the keeping of my aids.
No quota, bribe, initiation fee!

No one has ever asked for his money back!
Geniuses, beauties, all the greatest wits
Have been our patrons! Once the show's begun
Small kids admitted for a mere two-bits!
Fear not, my friends! There's room for everyone!
Step forward, please! Make room for those in back!

II PROUST ON SKATES

THE WHIRLIGIG OF TIME

HORACE 1:25

They are fewer these days, those supple, suntanned boys
Whose pebbles tapped at your window, and your door
Swings less and less on its obliging hinges
For wildly importunate suitors. Fewer the cries
Of "Lydia, how can you sleep when I've got the hots?
I won't last out the night; let me get my rocks off."
Things have moved right along, and, behold, it's you
Who quails, like a shriveled whore, as they scorn and
     dodge you,
And the wind shrieks like a sex-starved thing in heat
As the moon goes dark and the mouth of your old dry
     vulva
Rages and hungers, and your worst, most ulcerous pain
Is knowing those sleek-limbed boys prefer the myrtle,
The darling buds of May, leaving dried leaves
To cluster in unswept corners, fouling doorways.

A RUMINANT

As Sir Osbert Sitwell has remarked,
human beings display "the identical
combination of flaming pride and meek
submission that in the animal world
distinguishes the camel."

MARTIN C. D'ARCY, S.J.
The Mind and Heart of Love

Out of the Urdu, into our instant ken,
ambles the gross molester of the Sphinx,
    our *oont,* or camel,
hunchbacked from failed exertions, poor Ur-Punch
and brigand-clown of Noah's passengers,
    the Hebrew *gimel*

for the deformity it's luck to touch.
Footpadded and austere, a temperance leader,
    he slumps in torpid
reverie over a sea of blistering dunes,
yet easily is tamed, the Britannica says,
    because he's stupid.

Beware his soulful glances that conceal
absence of thought and the ferocity
    of a seasoned bigot,
who nevertheless briefly became the bearer
of kings and spices, the royal pattern of patience,
    and wisdom's legate.

PROSPECTS

We have set out from here for the sublime
Pastures of summer shade and mountain stream;
I have no doubt we shall arrive on time.

Is all the green of that enameled prime
A snapshot recollection or a dream?
We have set out from here for the sublime

Without provisions, without one thin dime,
And yet, for all our clumsiness, I deem
It certain that we shall arrive on time.

No guidebook tells you if you'll have to climb
Or swim. However foolish we may seem,
We have set out from here for the sublime

And must get past the scene of an old crime
Before we falter and run out of steam,
Riddled by doubt that we'll arrive on time.

Yet even in winter a pale paradigm
Of birdsong utters its obsessive theme.
We have set out from here for the sublime;
I have no doubt we shall arrive on time.

FOR JAMES MERRILL: AN ADIEU

As fadeth Sommers-sunne from gliding fountaines

The daily press keeps up-to-date obits
Cooling in morgues and is piously prepared
For the claim that any day may be one's last.
Dictators, famous short-stops, felons, wits
Intimately recline in darkly shared
Beds of fine print, their leaden, predestined past.

But you, dear friend, managed to slip away,
Actually disappear in the dead of winter
More perfectly than Yeats. As at a show,
While we were savoring all your skills, the play
Of your words, your elegant, serious banter,
You cloaked yourself, vanished like Prospero

Or Houdini, escaping from cold padlocked fact,
Manacles, blindfolds, all our earthly ties,
And there we sat, the master illusionist
Leaving us stunned in the middle of his act,
The stage vacant, expecting some surprise
Reentry from the wings to a rousing Liszt

Fanfare, tumultuous applause, a bow
And a gentle, pleased, self-deprecating smile.
There comes no manager hither to explain.
Words fail us, from the weak and fatuous "ciao,
Bello," to the bellowing grand style,
As we shuffle out to the shabby street and the rain.

You are now one of that chosen band and choice
Fellowship gathered at Sandover's sunlit end,
Fit audience though few, where, at their ease,
Dante, Rilke, Mallarmé, Proust rejoice
In the rich polyphony of their latest friend,
Scored in his sweetly noted higher keys.

SISTERS

How like a golden floating benediction
The morning sunlight loiters among leaves,
Emblazons tossing billows of gnats, unhives
Its honeyed treasure, and confers election

Upon all souls, on every blessed one
Here in this compound proctored by St. Vincent
De Paul in marble patience, and with ambient
Warmth anoints each blossom, twig and stone,

And the poor, baffled patients, shy as gerbils,
Hemmed in like helpless pets. They wander here
Over clipped lawns and through delicious air
In a second childhood, having lost their marbles.

One of them writes home to her elder brother,
"We had a birthday out in the violent ward.
I won a prize. The craziest can't play cards.
It's all they can do to converse about the weather.

Wouldn't you buy me a small graphaphone?
It wouldn't cost more than ten or twenty dollars,
Would it? A few old discs might serve as healers:
Stardust, perhaps, *Deep Purple, All My Own.*

We could dance to them and have some pleasant times.
It's allowed, I think. And the sisters wouldn't mind
If the music wasn't church but some good band.
(I'd want the smallest graphaphone that comes.)"

And the youngest nurses, made beautiful with care,
Sisters of Charity, escort the feeble
Through inward terrors, through memories that disable,
From dark brown hallways out into morning air,

To agate swirls and citrines of the sun,
Sparrows at their dust-baths, shameless, surprising
These scrubbed, diligent girls, their starched coifs rising
Like spinnakers, flame-white tongues of cyclamen.

THE MESSAGE

Fuscus, my friend, go tell that lying . . . Wait!
Hold on a moment. Let me reformulate
The sort of thing I'm after. Tell her she,
Whether she likes the thought or not, will be . . .
Or, rather, let me put it another way.
Say that you left me reveling, and say
Everyone says how good-natured I am.
And let her know I'm happy as a clam.

THE MYSTERIES OF CAESAR

Known to the boys in his Latin class as "Sir,"
Balding, cologned, mild-mannered Mr. Sypher
Defied his sentence as a highschool lifer
With a fresh, carefully chosen boutonniere

As daily he heard the Helvetians plead their cause
In chains while captives were brought face to face
With the impositions of the ablative case,
The torts and tortures of grammatic laws.

Gracelessly stalled by vast impediments
Of words and baggage as by a conqueror's shackles,
O'Rourke, his face a celestial sphere of freckles
(One Gaul brought down by the pluperfect tense)

Submitted to all the galls and agonies
Of pained sight-readings from the *Gallic Wars.*
They all bore dark, dishonorable scars
From what their textbook called an "exercise"

At least as draining as the quarter-mile.
But Mr. Sypher listened with superb
Imperial hauteur, with imperturb-
able patience, and a somewhat cryptic smile.

"Thompson," he'd murmur, "please instruct our class."
And Thompson would venture, timidly, much rattled,
"Caesar did withhold his men from battle,
And he did have enough in presentness

To prohibit the enemy from further wastings,
From foragings and rapines." And through a long
Winter campaign of floundering, grief, and wrong,
That little army force-marched without resting.

"Please aid us, Jones," Mr. Sypher would beseech;
And Jones would tremulously undertake
To decipher the old Caesarian mystique
In the mixed medium of cracked parts of speech.

"Which things being known, when surest things accede,
He did deem enough of cause . . . ," Jones volunteered.
Invariably it came out sounding weird,
The garbled utterance of some lesser breed

Without the law of common intercourse.
Long weeks of rain, followed by early frost
Had not improved morale, and yet the worst
Is not when there can always still be worse.

They rather liked Mr. Sypher, who was kind,
An easy grader. Was he a widower?
It was thought he had lost a child some years before.
Often they wondered what passed through his mind

As he calmly attended to their halt and crude
Efforts, not guessing one or another boy
Served as Antinous to that inward eye
Which is the pitiless bliss of solitude.

TO FORTUNA PARVULORUM

> *Young men have strong passions, and tend*
> *to gratify them indiscriminately ... they*
> *show absence of self-control ... they are hot*
> *tempered. Their lives are mainly spent not*
> *in memory but in expectation ... The*
> *character of Elderly Men [is different]. They*
> *have lived many years; they have often been*
> *taken in, and often made mistakes; and life*
> *on the whole is a bad business.*
>
> ARISTOTLE, *Rhetoric*, II, 12.

As a young man I was headstrong, willful, rash,
    Determined to amaze,
Grandly indifferent to comfort as to cash,
Past Envy's sneer, past Age's toothless gnash,
    Boldly I went my ways.

Then I matured. I sacrificed the years
    Lost in impetuous folly
To calm Prudentia, paying my arrears
For heedlessness in the cautious coin of fears
    And studious melancholy.

Now, having passed the obligatory stations,
    I turn in turn to you,
Divinity of diminished expectations,
To whom I direct these tardy supplications,
    Having been taught how few

Are blessed enough to encounter on their way
    The least chipped glint of joy,
And learned in what altered tones I hear today
The remembered words, *"Messieurs, les jeux sont faits,"*
    That stirred me as a boy.

A PLEDGE

Beauty of face, of body, and of spirit
Join with such grace in her of whom I write
No dreams of man or woman might come near it;
Yet she is wed, in heaven or hell's despite,
To an ignoble, titled troglodyte
For whom our pitiful language has no words
Sufficiently uncouth and impolite.
The air is sweetest that a thistle guards.

He'd have that lady's mind-inspiring merit
Kept secret, all her virtues out of sight,
Imprisoned in his castle's tallest turret,
His bushel basket stifling all her light,
Insensible of inwit's agenbite.
She who deserves the homages of bards
Languishes a neglected Shulamite.
The air is sweetest that a thistle guards.

But her great worth, beyond the count of karat,
Shall not be his alone if appetite,
Wit and determination may secure it.
Devotion such as mine must claim its right.
Gaul, like the afterlife, is tripartite,
And this ménage will shake down into thirds.
Odors of myrrh and nard invade the night.
The air is sweetest that a thistle guards.

Duke, you are unaware of your true plight;
Antlers and scorn for you are in the cards.
I have a yearning she shall yet requite:
The air is sweetest that a thistle guards.

THE LIFE OF CRIME

Burdened from birth with a lean Methodist
Father in daily touch with the Sublime,
It was small wonder I should turn to crime
As, of all methods to survive, the best.

Had I not often witnessed how a few
Spasmodic yeas and epigastric glories
Delivered inveterate sinners of all their worries,
Transported hopeless scoundrels from the pew

Of sin to the very otto of sanctity?
How refreshing it was, this early morning dip
In the Blood of the Lamb—how tempting to swim a
    lap,
Then shower and change before the *réchauffé*

Of habitual vice. Still, at an early age
I implored my father to be permitted to see
Kinkaid's New Travelling Menagerie,
Dreamed of as the Arabian cortège

That accompanied Melchior and Balthazar
To the crib from exotic ziggurat pavilions.
This was the era before my great rebellion,
When father and son had hopes for one another.

And then the day came. I could actually tell,
Before seeing the cages, flags, and tents,
The presence of those lithe inhabitants
Of Ali Baba's kingdom by their smell:

A strong sexual musk, filling the lung
With heated bestial vigor. Bales of straw
Scattered beneath the strut of hoof and paw
Mingled their scent with the raw odor of dung

As an incontestable presence and true sign
Of the animals I was about to see.
But as we entered, father lectured me
On the real nature of this nomadic shrine.

The camel was God's symbol for the grace
Of patience, never mind his sorrowful eyes;
The lion God's assurance we shall rise
Like Gospeler Mark from this polluted place.

And so to him the panther, the baboon,
Giraffe and walrus all were allegories,
Dim shapes enacting hobbled moral stories,
Denied even their smells that all too soon

Thinned and departed, like the Christmas kings,
Their turbans fine as smoke, their lives a tale
Told to instruct a child. The world, turned pale,
Exposed an absence at the core of things.

It was not long before I found I loathed
The pastor and his self-absolving flock,
And prided myself when I had learned to pick
The pockets of all the elegantly clothed.

LÀ-BAS: A TRANCE

From silk route Samarkand, emeralds and drugs
Find their way west, smuggled by leather-capped
Bandits with lard-greased hair across unmapped
Storm-tossed sand oceans drained to the very dregs,

And thence to such ports of call as Amsterdam,
The waters of its intricate canals
Gold-leafed and amethyst-shadowed by the veils
Of cloud-occluded suns, imaged in dim

Hempen mirages and opium reveries
Crowding the mind of a Parisian poet
With jasmine adornments to his barren garret,
The masts of frigates from all seven seas

Moored just outside his window, their bright rigging
What all his neighbors know as laundry lines.
France is as nothing; France and her finest wines
For all this fellow's interest can go begging

As the doors of his perception open wide
Admitting nothing but those nacreous errors
Harvested from unfathomed depths of mirrors:
Harems of young, voluptuous, sloe-eyed

Houris, undressed, awaiting his commands,
Untiring courtyard fountains casting jewels
Thriftlessly into blue-and-white-tiled pools,
Their splashes mingled with languid sarabandes.

Carpaccio's Middle East evokes an air-borne
Carpet, a sash and headgear the color of flame
Turned into Holland's tulips whose very name
Comes to him from the Turkish word for turban.

MATISSE: BLUE INTERIOR WITH TWO GIRLS—1947

... he lived through some of the most traumatic political events of recorded history, the worst wars, the greatest slaughters, the most demented rivalries of ideology, without, it seems, turning a hair.... Perhaps Matisse did suffer from fear and loathing like the rest of us, but there is no trace of them in his work. His studio was a world within a world: a place of equilibrium that, for sixty continuous years, produced images of comfort, refuge, and balanced satisfaction.

ROBERT HUGHES, *The Shock of the New*

Outside is variable May, a lawn of immediate green,
   The tree as blue as its shadow.
      A shutter angles out in charitable shade.
It is a world of yearning: we yearn for it,
   Its youthful natives yearn for one another.
      Their flesh is firm as a plum, their smooth
        tanned waists,
Lit through the fluttered leaves above their heads,
   Are rubbed and cinctured with this morning's
        bangles.
      Yet each, if we but take thought, is a lean gnomon,
A bone finger with its moral point:
   The hour, the minute, the dissolving pleasure.
      (Light fails, the shadows pool themselves in
        hollows.)
Here, in the stifling fragrance of mock orange,
   In the casual glance, the bright lust of the eye,
      Lies the hot spring of inevitable tears.

Within is the cool blue perfect cube of thought.
   The branched spirea carefully arranged
      Is no longer random growth: it now becomes

The object of our thought, it becomes our thought.
    The room is a retreat in which the drone
        Of the electric fan is modest, unassertive,
Faithful, as with a promise of lemonade
    And other gentle solaces of summer,
        Among which, for the two serene young girls
In this cool tank of blue is an open book
    Where they behold the pure unchanging text
        Of manifold, reverberating depth,
Quiet and tearless in its permanence.
    Deep in their contemplation the two girls,
        Regarding art, have become art themselves.
Once out of nature, they have settled here
    In this blue room of thought, beyond the reach
        Of the small brief sad ambitions of the flesh.

PROUST ON SKATES

*He stayed in bed, and at the beginning of
October still wasn't getting up till two in
the afternoon. But he made a seventy-mile
journey to Chamonix to join Albu* [Louis
Albufera] *and Louisa* [de Mornand,
Albufera's beautiful mistress] *on a
mule-back excursion to Montanvert, where
they went skating.*

RONALD HAYMAN
Proust: A Biography

The alpine forests, like huddled throngs of mourners,
Black, hooded, silent, resign themselves to wait
    As long as may be required;
A low pneumonia mist covers the glaciers,
Spruces are bathed in a cold sweat, the late
    Sun has long since expired,

Though barely risen, and the gray cast of the day
Is stark, unsentimental, and metallic.
    Earth-stained and chimney-soiled
Snow upon path and post is here to stay,
Foundered in endless twilight, a poor relic
    Of a once gladder world.

Sparse café patrons can observe a few
Skaters skimming the polished soapstone lake,
    A platform for their skill
At crosscut, grapevine, loop and curlicue,
Engelmann's Star, embroideries that partake
    Of talent, coaching, drill,

While a few tandem lovers, hand in hand,
Perform their *pas de deux* along the edges,
    Oblivious, unconcerned.
This is a stony, vapor-haunted land

Of granite dusk, of wind sieved by the hedges,
    Their branches braced and thorned.

Escaped from the city's politics and fribble,
Hither has come an odd party of three,
    Braided by silken ties:
With holiday abandon, the young couple
Have retreated into the deep privacy
    Of one another's eyes,

While the third, who in different ways yet loves them
        both,
Finds himself now, as usual, all alone,
    And lacing on his skates,
Steadies himself, cautiously issues forth
Into the midst of strangers and his own
    Interior debates.

Sweatered and mufflered to protect the weak
And lacey branches of his bronchial tree
    From the fine-particled threat
Of the moist air, he curves in an oblique
And gentle gradient, floating swift and free—
    No *danseur noble*, and yet

He glides with a gaining confidence, inscribes
Tentative passages, thinks again, backtracks,
    Comes to a minute point,
Then wheels about in widening sweeps and lobes,
Large Palmer cursives and smooth *entrelacs*,
    Preoccupied, intent

On a subtle, long-drawn style and pliant script
Incised with twin steel blades and qualified
    Perfectly to express,

With arms flung wide or gloved hands firmly gripped
Behind his back, attentively, clear-eyed,
    A glancing happiness.

It will not last, that happiness; nothing lasts;
But will reduce in time to the clear brew
    Of simmering memory
Nourished by shadowy gardens, music, guests,
Childhood affections, and, of Delft, a view
    Steeped in a sip of tea.

A DEATH IN WINTER

In memory of Joseph Brodsky,
born May 24, 1940, Leningrad;
died January 28, 1996, Brooklyn

Delicate sensors registered the shock,
Cool scanners shuddered but went unobserved;
It was very dark, of course, the city scarved
In the sleeping death of each day's life, each clock

Reckoning that brief moment only in passing.
Historian, watchman, made their careful note
Of power surges and ebbs, who's in, who's out.
At the hourly Bellevue bed-check no one was missing.

But this tremor, beyond the ten-tone Richter scale,
Unsettles us more, with its quiet ultra-sound,
Than cold tectonic plates, the underground
Turning of coats and strata, the old turmoil

And trepidation of societies and spheres.
Spaces are mourners. Prospect Park is the first
To cloak itself in darkness. Well rehearsed,
The Nevsky Prospect blacks out, disappears,

And before St. Mark's, the whole world's living room
Empties and floats away (as the spirit does)
With its pigeons and its tiny orchestras,
While the Luxembourg's stone gentry pace and roam

In solitary grief. Time itself mourns,
Going back to the same hour as if in search,
Time and again, of bedroom, study, porch,
In nightly, demented, desperate returns,

Looking for something lost, a loss untold,
Greater than many of us understand.
In the Republic of Letters one fine hand,
Cyrillic, cursive, American, has been stilled.

Survivor of show trial, of state oppression,
Exiled from parents, language, neighborhood,
This man's was the lasting sovereignty of the word,
Beyond the grasp of politics or fashion,

The hawk's domain and climate, whose largesse
Comes as a gift of snow from the obscure
Mid-winter gray in verse precise and pure.
He now dwells in the care of each of us.

Reader, dwell with his poems. Underneath
Their gaiety and music, note the chilled strain
Of irony, of felt and mastered pain,
The sound of someone laughing through clenched
   teeth.

THE DARKNESS AND THE LIGHT

For HELEN
and
In Memory of Harry and Kathleen Ford
and of William and Emily Maxwell

Aye, on the shores of darkness there is light.
JOHN KEATS

The exceeding brightness of this early sun
Makes me conceive how dark I have become,
. . . .
Oh! Rabbi, rabbi, fend my soul for me
And true savant of this dark nature be.
WALLACE STEVENS

LATE AFTERNOON: THE ONSLAUGHT OF LOVE

At this time of day
One could hear the caulking irons sound
Against the hulls in the dockyard.
Tar smoke rose between trees
And large oily patches floated on the water,
Undulating unevenly
In the purple sunlight
Like the surfaces of Florentine bronze.

At this time of day
Sounds carried clearly
Through hot silences of fading daylight.
The weedy fields lay drowned
In odors of creosote and salt.
Richer than double-colored taffeta,
Oil floated in the harbor,
Amoeboid, iridescent, limp.
It called to mind the slender limbs
Of Donatello's *David.*

It was lovely and she was in love.
They had taken a covered boat to one of the islands.
The city sounds were faint in the distance:
Rattling of carriages, tumult of voices,
Yelping of dogs on the decks of barges.

At this time of day
Sunlight empurpled the world.
The poplars darkened in ranks
Like imperial servants.
Water lapped and lisped
In its native and quiet tongue.
Oakum was in the air and the scent of grasses.
There would be fried smelts and cherries and cream.
Nothing designed by Italian artisans
Would match this evening's perfection.
The puddled oil was a miracle of colors.

CIRCLES

Long inventories of miseries unspoken,
Appointment books of pain,
Attars of love gone rancid, the pitcher broken
At the fountain, rooted unkindnesses:
All were implied by her, by me suspected,
At her saying, "I could not bear
Ever returning to that village in Maine.
For me the very air,
The harbor smells, the hills, all are infected."

I gave my sympathy, filled in the blanks
With lazy, bitter fictions,
And, feeling nothing, won her grateful thanks.

Many long years and some attachments later
I was to be instructed by the courts
Upon the nicest points of such afflictions,
Having become a weakened, weekend father.
All of us, in our own circle of hell
(Not that of forger, simonist or pander),
Patrolled the Olmsted bosks of Central Park,
Its children-thronged resorts,
Pain-tainted ground,
Where the innocent and the fallen join to play
In the fields, if not of the Lord, then of the Law;
Which decreed that love be hobbled and confined
To Saturday,
Trailing off into Sunday-before-dark;

And certain sandpits, slides, swings, monkey bars
Became the old thumbscrews of spoiled affection
And agonized aversion.
Of these, the most tormenting
In its single-songed, maddening monotony,
Its glaring-eyed and nostril-flaring steeds
With perfect teeth, but destined never to win
Their countless and interminable races,
Was the merry, garish, mirthless carousel.

MEMORY

Sepia oval portraits of the family,
Black-framed, adorned the small brown-papered hall,
But the parlor was kept unused, never disturbed.
Under a glass bell, the dried hydrangeas
Had bleached to the hue of ancient newspaper,
Though once, someone affirmed, they had been pink.
Pink still were the shiny curling orifices
Of matching seashells stationed on the mantel
With mated, spiked, wrought-iron candlesticks.
The room contained a tufted ottoman,
A large elephant-foot umbrella stand
With two malacca canes, and two peacock
Tail-feathers sprouting from a small-necked vase.
On a teak side table lay, side by side,
A Bible and a magnifying glass.
Green velvet drapes kept the room dark and airless
Until on sunny days toward midsummer
The brass andirons caught a shaft of light
For twenty minutes in late afternoon
In a radiance dimly akin to happiness—
The dusty gleam of temporary wealth.

MIRROR

for J. D. McClatchy

Always halfway between you and your double,
Like Washington, I cannot tell a lie.
When the dark queen demands in her querulous treble,
"Who is the fairest?," inaudibly I reply,

"Beauty, your highness, dwells in the clouded cornea
Of the self-deceived beholder, whereas Truth,
According to film moguls of California,
Lies in makeup, smoke and mirrors, gin and vermouth,

Or the vinous second-pressings of *Veritas*,
Much swilled at Harvard. The astronomer's speculum
Reveals it, and to the politician's cheval glass
It's that part of a horse he cannot distinguish from

His elbow; but it's also the upside-down
Melodies of Bach fugues, the right-to-left
Writing of Leonardo, a long-term loan
From Hebrew, retrograde fluencies in deft,

Articulate penmanship. An occasional Louis
Might encounter it in the corridors of Versailles;
It evades the geometrician's confident QE
D, but the constant motion from ground to sky

And back again of the terrible Ferris wheel
Sackville describes in *A Mirror for Magistrates*
Conveys some semblance of the frightening feel
Of the mechanical heartlessness of Fate,

The ring-a-ding-*Ding-an-Sich*. Yet think how gaily
In the warped fun-house glass our flesh dissolves
In shape and helpless laughter, unlike the Daily
Mirror in which New Yorkers saw themselves.

It's when no one's around that I'm most truthful,
In a world as timeless as before The Fall.
No one to reassure that she's still youthful,
I gaze untroubled at the opposite wall.

Light fades, of course, with the oncoming of dusk;
I faithfully note the rheostat dial of day
That will rise to brilliance, weaken as it must
Through each uncalibrated shade of gray,

One of them that of winter afternoons,
Desolate, leaden, and in its burden far
Deeper than darkness, engrossing in its tones
Those shrouded regions where the meanings are."

SAMSON

There came to the nameless wife of Manoah
In annunciation an angel who declared:
"Like Sarah who was barren, even so shall you
Conceive a child; you also shall bear a son."

    Almost every day at the Boston Lying-In
    There are births defying expectation, all
    Medical wisdom; almost daily a mother thinks
    Her child God-given, a miracle and a wonder.

And the angel said: "You must both abstain from wine,
You and the child; from all contact with the dead;
Nor let your hair be shorn, for he is God's,
And he shall be a Nazarite from the womb."

    In the Hebrew shul at Lodz the little boys
    Studied the Torah, and let their sidelocks curl
    And sway to the rhythm of reading. They too
       have been
    Sacrificed, like Nazarites before them.

AN ORPHIC CALLING

for Mihaly Csikszentmihalyi

The stream's *courante* runs on, a *force majeure,*
A Major rippling of the pure mind of Bach,
Tumult of muscled currents, formed in far
Reaches of edelweiss, cloud and alpenstock,

Now folding into each other, flexing, swirled
In cables of perdurable muscle-tones,
Hurrying through this densely noted world,
Small chambers, studio mikes, Concorde headphones,

And from deep turbulent rapids, roiled and spun,
They rise in watery cycles to those proud
And purifying heights where they'd begun
On Jungfrau cliffs of edelweiss and cloud,

Piled cumuli, that *fons et origo*
("Too lofty and original to rage")
Of the mind's limpid unimpeded flow
Where freedom and necessity converge

And meet in a fresh curriculum of love
(Minor in grief, major in happiness)
As interlocking melodies contrive
Small trysts and liaisons, briefly digress

But only to return to Interlaken
Altitudes of clear trebles, crystal basses,
Fine reconciliations and unbroken
Threadings of fern-edged flutes down tumbling races.

An Orphic calling it is, one that invites
Responsories, a summons to lute-led
Nature, as morning's cinnabar east ignites
And the instinctive sunflower turns its head.

RARA AVIS IN TERRIS

for Helen

Hawks are in the ascendant. Just look about.
Cormorants, ravens, jailbirds of ominous wing
Befoul the peace, their caws
                              raised in some summoning
    To an eviscerating cause,
    Some jihad, some rash all-get-out
Crusade, leaving the field all gore and guano
Justified in hysterical soprano

By balding buzzards who brandish the smart bomb,
The fractured atom in their unclipped talons.
Ruffling with all the pride
                              of testosteronic felons,
    They storm the airwaves with implied
    Threats and theatrical aplomb
Or cruise the sky with delta stealth and gelid
Chestsful of combat-decorative fruit salad.

It's the same in the shady groves of academe:
Cold eye and primitive beak and callused foot
Conjunctive to destroy
                              all things of high repute,
    Whole epics, Campion's songs, Tolstoy,
    Euclid and logic's enthymeme,
As each man bares his scalpel, whets his saber,
As though enjoined to deconstruct his neighbor.

And that's not the worst of it; there are the Bacchae,
The ladies' auxiliary of the raptor clan
With their bright cutlery,
                              sororal to a man.
     And feeling peckish, they foresee
     An avian banquet in the sky,
Feasting off dead white European males,
Or local living ones, if all else fails.

But where are the mild monogamous lovebirds,
     Parakeets, homing pigeons, sundry doves,
Beringed, bewitching signs
                              of the first, greatest loves
     Eros or Agape gently defines?
     God's for the ark's small flocks and herds,
Or Venus incarnate as that quasi-queen
Of France known as Diane de la Poitrine.

They are here, my dear, they are here in the marble
     air,
     According to the micro-Mosaic law,
Miraculously aloft
                              above that flood and flaw
     Where Noah darkly plies his craft.
     Lightly an olive branch they bear,
Its deathless leafage emblematic of
A quarter-century of faultless love.

A FALL

Those desolate, brute, chilling sublimities,
Unchanging but as the light may chance to fall,
Deserts of snow, forlorn barrens of rock,
What could be more indifferent to man's life
Than your average Alp, stripped to the blackened bone
Above the tree line, except where the ice rags,
Patches, and sheets of winter cling yearlong?
The cowbell's ludicrous music, the austere
Sobrieties of Calvin, precision watches,
A cheese or two, and that is all the Swiss
Have given the world, unless we were to cite
The questionable morals of their banks.
But how are people to live in dignity
When at two p.m. the first shadows of night,
Formed by the massive shoulder of some slope,
Cast, for the rest of the day, entire valleys—
Their window boxes of geraniums,
Their cobbles, pinecones, banners and coffee cups—
Into increasing sinks and pools of dark?
And that is but half the story. The opposing slope
Keeps morning from its flaxen charities
Until, on midsummer days, eleven-thirty,
When fresh birdsong and cow dung rinse the air
And all outdoors still glistens with night-dew.
All this serves to promote a state of mind
Cheerless and without prospects. But yesterday
I let myself, in spite of dark misgivings,

Be talked into a strenuous excursion
Along one high ridge promising a view.
And suddenly, at a narrowing of the path,
The whole earth fell away, and dizzily
I beheld the most majestic torrent in Europe,
A pure cascade, over six hundred feet,
Falling straight down—it was like Rapunzel's hair,
But white, as if old age and disappointment
Had left her bereft of suitors. Down it plunged,
Its great, continuous, unending weight
Toppling from above in a long shaft
Or carven stem that broke up at its base
Into enormous rhododendron blooms
Of spray, a dense array of shaken blossoms.
I teetered perilously, scared and dazed,
And slowly, careful of both hand and foot,
Made my painstaking way back down the trail.
That evening in my bedroom I recalled
The scene's terror and grandeur, my vertigo
Mixed with a feeling little short of awe.
And I retraced my steps in the secure
Comfort of lamplight on a Baedeker.
That towering waterfall I just had viewed
At what had seemed the peril of my life
Was regarded locally with humorous
Contempt, and designated the *Pisse-Vache.*

HAMAN

I am Haman the Hangman, the engineer
And chief designer of that noble structure,
The Gallows. Let the Jews tremble and beware:
I have made preparations for their capture
And extirpation in a holy war
Against their foolish faith, their hateful culture,
An ethnic cleansing that will leave us pure,
Ridding the world of this revolting creature.
I shall have camps, *Arbeit Macht Frei*, the lure
Of hope, the chastening penalty of torture,
And other entertainments of despair,
The which I hanker after like a lecher.
And best of all, the gibbet, my friend, my poor
One-armed assistant, in stiff, obedient posture,
Like a young officer's salute, but more
Rigid, and more instructive than a lecture,
Saying, "I can teach you to tread on air,
And add another cubit to your stature."

A CERTAIN SLANT

Etched on the window were barbarous thistles of frost,
Edged everywhere in that tame winter sunlight
With pavé diamonds and fine prickles of ice
Through which a shaft of the late afternoon
Entered our room to entertain the sway
And float of motes, like tiny aqueous lives,
Then glanced off the silver teapot, raising stains
Of snailing gold upcast across the ceiling,
And bathed itself at last in the slop bucket
Where other aqueous lives, equally slow,
Turned in their sad, involuntary courses,
Swiveled in eel-green broth. Who could have known
Of any elsewhere? Even of out-of-doors,
Where the stacked firewood gleamed in drapes of glaze
And blinded the sun itself with jubilant theft,
The smooth cool plunder of celestial fire?

A BRIEF ACCOUNT OF OUR CITY

for Dorothea Tanning

If you approach our city from the south,
The first thing that you'll see is the Old Fort,
High on its rock. Its crenellated walls,
Dungeons and barbicans and towers date back
To the eighth century. The local barons
Of hereditary title moved their courts
Inside whenever they were under siege
With all their retinues, taxing the poor,
Feuding with neighboring baronies, masterful
Only in greed and management of arms.
Great murderous vulgar men, they must have been.
The fort, history records, was never taken.
It might be worth a visit when you come.
For a mere thirty kroner you can ascend
The turrets for a quite incomparable view.
From there our forests look a lot like parsley
And cress; there the wind enters your throat
Like an iced mountain stream. Piled here and there
You will find pyramids of cannonballs
In the great courtyard, stacked like croquembouches,
Warm to the touch where the sun glances off them
And chilly in the shade. The arsenal,
Containing arquebuses, fruitwood bows,
As well as heavy mortars and great cannons,

Is open to the public. The furniture
Is solid, thick and serviceable stuff,
No nonsense. But what may strike you most of all
Is the plain, barren spareness of the rooms.
No art here. Nothing to appease the eye.
And not because such things have been removed
To our museums. This was the way they lived:
In self-denying, plain austerity.
As you draw nearer to the city itself
You will make out, beyond the citadel,
The shapely belfry of Our Lady of Sorrows.
Then you will see, in the midst of a great field,
Surrounded on all sides by acres of wheat,
A large, well-cared-for, isolated house—
No others neighboring, or even within view—
Which is given free of charge by the city board
To the Public Executioner. His children
Are allowed a special tutor, but not admitted
To any of our schools. The family
Can raise all that's required for their meals
Right on the grounds, and, if need be, a doctor
Will call on them, given half a day's notice.
The children are forbidden to leave the place,
As is, indeed, the entire family,
Except when the father alone is called upon
To perform official duties. And by this means
Everyone is kept happy; our citizens
Need have no fear of encountering any of them,

While they live comfortably at our expense.
Whenever you visit, be certain that you dine
At one of our fine restaurants; don't miss
The Goldene Nockerl, which for potato dumplings
Cannot be matched, and our rich amber beer
Is widely known as the finest in this region.

SAUL AND DAVID

It was a villainous spirit, snub-nosed, foul
Of breath, thick-taloned and malevolent,
That squatted within him wheresoever he went
    And possessed the soul of Saul.

There was no peace on pillow or on throne.
In dreams the toothless, dwarfed, and squinny-eyed
Started a joyful rumor that he had died
    Unfriended and alone.

The doctors were confounded. In his distress, he
Put aside arrogant ways and condescended
To seek among the flocks where they were tended
    By the youngest son of Jesse,

A shepherd boy, but goodly to look upon,
Unnoticed but God-favored, sturdy of limb
As Michelangelo later imagined him,
    Comely even in his frown.

Shall a mere shepherd provide the cure of kings?
Heaven itself delights in ironies such
As this, in which a boy's fingers would touch
    Pythagorean strings

And by a modal artistry assemble
The very Sons of Morning, the ranked and choired
Heavens in sweet laudation of the Lord,
      And make Saul cease to tremble.

DESPAIR

Sadness. The moist gray shawls of drifting sea-fog,
Salting scrub pine, drenching the cranberry bogs,
Erasing all but foreground, making a ghost
Of anyone who walks softly away;
And the faint, penitent psalmody of the ocean.

Gloom. It appears among the winter mountains
On rainy days. Or the tiled walls of the subway
In caged and aging light, in the steel scream
And echoing vault of the departing train,
The vacant platform, the yellow destitute silence.

But despair is another matter. Midafternoon
Washes the worn bank of a dry arroyo,
Its ocher crevices, unrelieved rusts,
Where a startled lizard pauses, nervous, exposed
To the full glare of relentless marigold sunshine.

THE HANGING GARDENS OF TYBURN

Mysteriously fed by the dying breath
Of felons, by the foul odor that melts
Down from their bodies hanging on the gallows,
The rank, limp flesh, the soft pendulous guilts,

This solitary plant takes root at night,
Its tiny charnel blossoms the pale blue
Of Pluto's ice pavilions; being dried,
Powdered and mixed with the cold morning dew

From the left hand of an executed man,
It confers untroubled sleep, and can prevent
Prenatal malformations if applied
To a woman's swelling body, except in Lent.

Take care to clip only the little blossoms,
For the plant, uprooted, utters a cry of pain
So highly pitched as both to break the eardrum
And render the would-be harvester insane.

JUDITH

It took less valor than I'm reputed for.
Since I was a small child I have hated men.
Even the feeblest, in their fantasies,
Triumph as sexual athletes, putting the shot
Squarely between the thighs of some meek woman,
While others strut like decathlon champions,
Like royal David hankering after his neighbor's
Dutiful wife. For myself, I found a husband
Not very prepossessing, but very rich.
Neither of us was interested in children.
In my case, the roving hands, the hot tumescence of
    an uncle,
Weakened my taste for close intimacies.
Ironically, heaven had granted me
What others took to be attractive features
And an alluring body, and which for years
Instinctively I looked upon with shame.
All men seemed stupid in their lecherous,
Self-flattering appetites, which I found repugnant.
But at last, as fate would have it, I found a chance
To put my curse to practical advantage.
It was easy. Holofernes was pretty tight;
I had only to show some cleavage and he was done for.

ILLUMINATION

Ground lapis for the sky, and scrolls of gold,
Before which shepherds kneel, gazing aloft
At visiting angels clothed in egg-yolk gowns,
Celestial tinctures smuggled from the East,
From sunlit Eden, the palmed and plotted banks
Of sun-tanned Aden. Brought home in fragile grails,
Planted in England, rising at Eastertide,
Their petals cup stamens of topaz dust,
The powdery stuff of cooks and cosmeticians.
But to the camel's-hair tip of the finest brush
Of Brother Anselm, it is the light of dawn,
Gilding the hems, the sleeves, the fluted pleats
Of the antiphonal archangelic choirs
Singing their melismatic *pax in terram.*
The child lies cribbed below, in bestial dark,
Pale as the tiny tips of crocuses
That will find their way to the light through drifts of
     snow.

LOOK DEEP

Look deep into my eyes. Think to yourself,
"There is 'the fringèd curtain' where a play
Will shortly be enacted." Look deep down
Into the pupil. Think, "I am going to sleep."

The pupil has its many-tinctured curtain
Of moiré silks, parted to let you in,
And the play will present a goddess you used to know
From the glint of sunlit fountain, from beveled mirror,

A goddess, yes, but only a messenger
Whose message is the armorial fleur-de-lys
She carries in her right hand, signifying
The majesty of France, as handed down

From the royal house of Solomon and David:
Wisdom, music and valor gracefully joined
In trefoil heraldry. Nearly asleep,
You settle down for a full-scale production

Of *The Rainstorm* in its grand entirety,
Which, greater than *The Ring*, lasts forty nights;
Everything huddled in one rocking stateroom,
A saving remnant, a life-raft-world in little.

Dream at your ease of the dark forests of spruce
Swaying in currents of green, gelatinous winds
Above which the classless zoo and zookeepers
Weather the testing and baptismal waters;

Dream of the long, undeviating gloom,
The unrelenting skies, the pounding wet
Through which a peak will thrust, a light, and over
The covenanted ark, an *arc-en-ciel.*

NOCTURNE: A RECURRING DREAM

The moon is a pearl in mist and sets the scene.
Comfort seems within reach, just over there,
But rocks, water, and darkness intervene.

Incalculable dangers lie between
Us and the warmth of bedding, the fire's flare.
The moon is a pearl in mist and sets the scene;

She's not, as claimed Ben Jonson, heaven's queen.
More ghostly, an omen of death hung in the air.
Rocks, water, and darkness intervene

Between that shadowy dwelling, barely seen,
And something not at all unlike despair.
The moon is a pearl in mist and sets the scene

For—secret rites? Ensorcellment? Marine
Catastrophe? Before we can declare,
Rocks, water, and darkness intervene.

Oystery pale, anything but serene,
Our goal seems cloaked in the forbidding glare
Of moonlight as a pearl that sets the scene
Where rocks, water, and darkness intervene.

LOT'S WIFE

How simple the pleasures of those childhood days,
Simple but filled with exquisite satisfactions.
The iridescent labyrinth of the spider,
Its tethered tensor nest of polygons
Puffed by the breeze to a little bellying sail—
Merely observing this gave infinite pleasure.
The sound of rain. The gentle graphite veil
Of rain that makes of the world a steel engraving,
Full of soft fadings and faint distances.
The self-congratulations of a fly,
Rubbing its hands. The brown bicameral brain
Of a walnut. The smell of wax. The feel
Of sugar to the tongue: a delicious sand.
One understands immediately how Proust
Might cherish all such postage-stamp details.
Who can resist the charms of retrospection?

PUBLIC GARDENS

"Flow'rs of all hue," a sightless Milton wrote
Of Paradise, which doesn't mean "all flowers."
An impoverished exile in his loneliest hours
Knows that not everybody makes the boat.

He has not mastered the language, he still retains
A craving for some remembered native dishes;
These sorrowful foreign skies, all smoke and ashes,
Remain uncleansed by the pummeling winter rains.

Jobless, he mopes in the shabby public gardens
Where importunate pigeons harry him for food.
Back in the dark unwelcome solitude
Of his attic room, he can view through the daisied
    curtains

The pantile roofs of this dirty little port.
But without passport or valid papers his fate
Lies with officials. Immense reasons of state
Conjoin to deny him permission to depart.

His is a sad but not uncommon lot,
Familiar to border guards, to police and such.
Even plantain, spleenwort, lichen, tuber and vetch
May be found in Paradise; the teasel not.

SACRIFICE

I *Abraham*

Long years, and I found favor
In the sight of the Lord, who brought me out of Ur
    To where his promise lay,
    There with him to confer
On Justice and Mercy and the appointed day
    Of Sodom's ashen fate;
For me he closeted sweetness in the date,
    And gave to salt its savor.

    Three promises he gave,
Came like three kings or angels to my door:
    His purposes concealed
    In coiled and kerneled store
He planted as a seedling that would yield
    In my enfeebled years
A miracle that would command my tears
    With piercings of the grave.

    "Old man, behold Creation,"
Said the Lord, "the leaping hills, the thousand-starred
    Heavens and watery floor.
    Is anything too hard
For the Lord, who shut all seas within their doors?"
    And then, for his name's sake
He led me, knowing where my heart would break,
    Into temptation.

The whole of my long life
Pivoted on one terrible day at dawn.
Isaac, my son, and I
Were to Moriah gone.
There followed an hour in which I wished to die,
Being visited by these things:
My name called out, the beat of gigantic wings,
Faggots, and flame, and knife.

II *Isaac*

Youthful I was and trusting and strong of limb,
The fresh-split firewood roped tight to my back,
And I bore unknowing that morning my funeral pyre.
My father, face averted, carried the flame,
And, in its scabbard, the ritual blade he bore.
It seemed to me at the time a wearisome trek.

I thought of my mother, how, in her age, the Lord
Had blessed her among women, giving her me
As joke and token both, unlikelihood
Being his way. But where, where from our herd
Was the sacrifice, I asked my father. He,
In a spasm of agony, bound me hand and foot.

I thought, *I am poured out like water, like wax
My heart is melted in the midst of my bowels.*
Both were tear-blinded. Hate and love and fear
Wrestled to ruin us, savage us beyond cure.
And the fine blade gleamed with the fury of live coals
Where we had reared an altar among the rocks.

Peace be to us both, to father Abraham,
To me, elected the shorn stunned lamb of God—
We were sentenced and reprieved by the same Voice—
And to all our seed, by this terror sanctified,
To be numbered even as the stars at the small price
Of an old scapegoated and thicket-baffled ram.

III *1945*

It was widely known that the army of occupation
Was in full retreat. The small provincial roads
Rumbled now every night with tanks and trucks,
Echoed with cries in German, much *mach schnell,*
Zurück, ganz richtig, augenblicklich, jawohl,
Audible in the Normandy countryside.
So it had been for days, or, rather, nights,
The troops at first making their moves in darkness,
But pressures of haste toward the end of March
Left stragglers to make their single ways alone,
At their own risk, and even in daylight hours.

Since the soldiers were commandeering anything
They needed—food, drink, vehicles of all sorts—
One rural family dismantled their bicycle,
Daubed the chrome parts—rims, sprocket, spokes—
    with mud,
And wired them carefully to the upper boughs
Of the orchard. And the inevitable came
In the shape of a young soldier, weighted down
With pack and bedroll, rifle, entrenching tools,
Steel helmet and heavy boots just after dawn.
The family was at breakfast. He ordered them out
In front of the house with abusive German words
They couldn't understand, but gesture and rifle

Made his imperious wishes perfectly clear.
They stood in a huddled group, all nine of them.
And then he barked his furious command:
Fahrrad! They all looked blank. He shouted again:
FAHRRAD! FAHRRAD! FAHRRAD!, as though sheer
    volume
Joined with his anger would make his meaning plain.
The father of the family experimentally
Inquired, *Manger?* The soldier, furious,
At last dredged up an explosive *Bicyclette,*
Proud of himself, contemptuous of them.
To this the father in a small pantomime—
Shrugged shoulders, palms turned out, a helpless, long,
Slow shaking of the head, then the wide gesture
Of an arm, taking in all his property—
Conveyed *Nous n'avons pas de bicyclettes*
More clearly than his words. To the young soldier
This seemed unlikely. No one could live this far
From neighbors, on a poor untraveled road
That lacked phone lines, without the usual means
Of transport. There was no time to search
The house, the barn, cowsheds, coops, pens and grounds.
He looked at the frightened family huddled together,
And with the blunt nose of his rifle barrel
Judiciously singled out the eldest son,
A boy perhaps fourteen, but big for his years,
Obliging him to place himself alone
Against the whitewashed front wall of the house.
Then, at the infallible distance of ten feet,

With rifle pointed right at the boy's chest,
The soldier shouted what was certainly meant
To be his terminal order: *BICYCLETTE!*

It was still early on a chilly morning.
The water in the tire-treads of the road
Lay clouded, polished pale and chalked with frost,
Like the paraffin-sealed coverings of preserves.
The very grass was a stiff lead-crystal gray,
Though splendidly prismatic where the sun
Made its slow way between the lingering shadows
Of nearby fence posts and more distant trees.
There was leisure enough to take full note of this
In the most minute detail as the soldier held
Steady his index finger on the trigger.

It wasn't charity. Perhaps mere prudence,
Saving a valuable round of ammunition
For some more urgent crisis. Whatever it was,
The soldier reslung his rifle on his shoulder,
Turned wordlessly and walked on down the road
The departed German vehicles had taken.

There followed a long silence, a long silence.
For years they lived together in that house,
Through daily tasks, through all the family meals,
In agonized, unviolated silence.

THE WITCH OF ENDOR

I had the gift, and arrived at the technique
That called up spirits from the vasty deep
To traffic with our tumid flesh, to speak
Of the unknown regions where the buried keep
Their counsel, but for such talents I was banned
By Saul himself from sortilege and spell
Who banished thaumaturges from the land
Where in their ignorance the living dwell.

But then he needed me; he was sore afraid,
And begged for forbidden commerce with the dead.
Samuel he sought, and I raised up that shade,
Laggard, resentful, with shawl-enfolded head,
Who spoke a terrible otherworldly curse
In a hollow, deep, engastrimythic voice.

INDOLENCE

Beyond the corruption both of rust and moth,
I loaf and invite my soul, calmly I slump
On the crowded sidewalk, blissed to the gills on hemp;
Mine is a sanctified and holy sloth.

The guilty and polluted come to view
My meek tranquility, the small tin cup
That sometimes runneth over. They fill it up
To assuage the torments they are subject to,

And hasten to the restoratives of sin,
While I, a flower-child, beautiful and good,
Remain inert, as St. Matthew said I should:
I rest, I toil not, neither do I spin.

Think how this sound economy of right
And wrong wisely allows me to confer
On all the bustling who in their bustling err
Consciences of a pure and niveous white.

THE ASHEN LIGHT OF DAWN

Reveille was bugled through army camps
As a soft dawn wind was fluttering streetlamps.

It was that hour when smooth sun-tanned limbs
Of adolescents twitched with unlawful dreams,
When, like a bloodshot eye beside the bed,
A nightlamp soaked oncoming day in red,
When, weighted beneath a humid body's brawn,
The soul mimicked that duel of lamp and dawn.
Like a face dried by the wind of recent tears,
The air is rife with whatever disappears,
And woman wearies of love, man of his chores.

Here and there chimneys smoked. The local whores,
Mascara'ed, overpainted, slept a stone
And stupid sleep, while the impoverished crone,
Breasts limp and frigid, alternately blew
On embers and on fingers, both going blue.
It was the hour of grief, of chill, of want;
Women in childbirth felt their seizures mount;
Like a thick, blood-choked scream, a rooster crowed
Distantly from some dim, befogged abode
As a sea of fog englutted the city blocks,
And in some seedy hospice, human wrecks
Breathed their death-rattling last, while debauchees
Tottered toward home, drained of their powers to
    please.

All pink and green in flounces, Aurora strolled
The vacant Seine embankments as the old,
Stupefied, blear-eyed Paris, glum and resigned,
Laid out his tools to begin the daily grind.

BAUDELAIRE

THE PLASTIC AND THE POETIC FORM

Let that Greek youth out of clay
   Mold an urn to fashion
Beauty, gladdening the eye
   With deft-handed vision.

But the poet's sterner test
   Urges him to seize on
A Euphrates of unrest,
   Fluid in evasion.

Duly bathed and cooled, his mind,
   Ardorless, will utter
Liquid song, his forming hand
   Lend a shape to water.

GOETHE

THE BEQUEST

Good folk, my love's abandoned me.
Whoever gets her, willingly
(Although she's kind as well as fair)
I give her to him as my heir,
Blithe, easy, unencumbered, free.

She wields her graces cunningly,
And God knows her fidelity.
Let him who wins her next take care.
Good folk, my love's abandoned me.

Let him look after her and see
She's kept from smirch and calumny
Because the darling thing might snare
Any man's heart who's unaware.
Forlorn I make my threnody:
Good folk, my love's abandoned me.

VAILLANT

ONCE MORE, WITH FEELING

The world has doffed her outerwear
Of chilling wind and teeming rain,
And donned embroidery again,
Tailored with sunlight's gilded flair.

No beast of field nor bird of air
But sings or bellows this refrain:
"The world has doffed her outerwear
Of chilling wind and teeming rain."

Fountain, millrace and river spare
No costly beading nor abstain
From silvered liveries of grosgrain.
All is new-clad and debonair.
The world has doffed her outerwear.

CHARLES D'ORLÉANS

LE JET D'EAU

My dear, your lids are weary;
Lower them, rest your eyes—
As though some languid pleasure
Wrought on you by surprise.
The tattling courtyard fountain
Repeats this night's excess
In fervent, ceaseless tremors
Of murmur and caress.

> A spray of petaled brilliance
> > That uprears
> In gladness as the Moon-
> > Goddess appears
> Falls like an opulent glistening
> > Of tears.

Even thus, your soul, exalted,
Primed by the body's joys,
Ascends in quenchless cravings
To vast, enchanted skies,
And then brims over, dying
In swoons, faint and inert,
And drains to the silent, waiting,
Dark basin of my heart.

A spray of petaled brilliance
    That uprears
In gladness as the Moon-
    Goddess appears
Falls like an opulent glistening
    Of tears.

You, whom the night makes radiant,
How amorous to lie, spent,
Against your breasts and listen
To the fountain's soft lament.
O Moon, melodious waters,
Wind-haunted trees in leaf,
Your melancholy mirrors
My ardors and their grief.

A spray of petaled brilliance
    That uprears
In gladness as the Moon-
    Goddess appears
Falls like an opulent glistening
    Of tears.

BAUDELAIRE

TAKING CHARGE

Back off, clear out, the lot of you,
Vile Melancholy, Spleen, and Woe;
Think you to dog me to and fro
As in the past you used to do?

Not anymore. "Begone. You're through,"
Says Reason, your determined foe.
Back off, clear out, the lot of you,
Vile Melancholy, Spleen, and Woe.

If you resurface, may God throw
You and your whole damnable crew
Back where you came from down below,
And thereby give the fiend his due.
Back off, clear out, the lot of you.

CHARLES D'ORLÉANS

A SYMPOSIUM

Only a Thracian goon would lurch from tippling
To brawling. Barbarians one and all. For our part
Let's preserve the rites of Bacchus, our seemly and civil
Devotions in the calm service of pleasure.
Good wine imbibed by lamplight has nothing to do
With bashed-in cups or swordplay. Subdue your clamor,
My friends, and use your well-connected elbows
For hoisting moderate drinks. You ask that I
Knock back my own full share of Falernian must.
Then let's hear Megylla's brother tell us who knocked
    him
All of a heap with the heavy weapons of bliss.
Suddenly tongue-tied? Well then, I'm swearing off,
Not a drop more. Those are my fixed conditions.
Whichever beauty it was that sent you reeling,
There's nothing to blush about, since you only go
For the classy and high-toned. Come on, just whisper
Her name in my ear.
                    O you poor silly kid,
You've bought yourself a regular Charybdis;
You deserve better. What can Thessalian spells,
Wizards or magic ointments do for you now?
Snagged by the tripartite, hybrid beast, Chimera,
Not even Bellerophon, mounted on Pegasus, could save
    you.

HORACE I.xxvii

A SPECIAL OCCASION

O *mise-en-bouteille* in the very year of my birth
And Manlius' consulship, celestial spirits,
Instinct with ardors, slugfests, the sighs of lovers,
Hilarity and effortless sleep, whatever,
Campanian harvest, well-sealed special reserve
For some fine and festive holiday, descend
From your high cellarage, since my friend Corvinus,
A connoisseur, has called for a more mature wine.
Soaked though he be in vintage Socratic wisdom,
He's not going to snub you. For even Cato the Elder,
All Roman rectitude, would warm to a drink.

You limber the dullard's faculties with your proddings;
With Bacchus the Trickster you break through careful
    discretion,
Making even the politic say what they mean.
You resurrect hope in the most dejected of minds;
To the poor and weak you lend such measure of courage
As after a single gulp allays their palsy
When faced with the wrath of monarchs, or
    unsheathed weapons.
Bacchus and Venus (if she will condescend),
The arm-linked Graces in unclad sorority,
And vigil lamps will honor you all night long
Till Phoebus, with punctual bustle, banishes starlight.

HORACE III.xxi

A PRAYER TO TWIN DIVINITIES

Let the girls sing of Diana in joyful praise
And the boys of her twin, Apollo unshorn, shall sing
And honor their sacred mother, whom Jupiter, king
Of gods, so favored, honor with song and the bays.

Of Diana let the girls sing, goddess of streams
Who loves the icy mountain, the darkened leafage
Of the Erymanthian woods, the brighter boscage
Of Lycian heights, young girls, give her your hymns.

To Tempe, to Phoebus Apollo's native isle
Give praise, you boys, and praise many times over
His godly shoulder slung with both lyre and quiver,
His brother's instrument, his festive, sacred soil.

Hearing your prayers, Apollo, god-begotten,
Will fend off war and plague and all ill omen
From Caesar and his people, and banish famine
To the lands of the barbarous Parthian and Briton.

HORACE I.xxi

MIRIAM

I had a nice voice once, and a large following.
I was, you might say, a star.
Of course, today, no one would ever know it.
My brothers have managed to corner all the attention
In spite of some rather dubious behavior.
O I could sing and dance with the best of them,
Pattern my feet to the jubilant hosannas.
But now I am always silent, always veiled,
Not only in public but in my private chambers
Where there are no mirrors or polished surfaces
In which my white affliction could be reflected.
I've even given up going through my scrapbooks;
The past is past; it's no good to anyone.
Many were lovely once, at least as children.

WITNESS

Against the enormous rocks of a rough coast
The ocean rams itself in pitched assault
And spastic rage to which there is no halt;
Foam-white brigades collapse; but the huge host

Has infinite reserves; at each attack
The impassive cliffs look down in gray disdain
At scenes of sacrifice, unrelieved pain,
Figured in froth, aquamarine and black.

Something in the blood-chemistry of life,
Unspeakable, impressive, undeterred,
Expresses itself without needing a word
In this sea-crazed Empedoclean Strife.

It is a scene of unmatched melancholy,
Weather of misery, cloud cover of distress,
To which there are no witnesses, unless
One counts the briny, tough and thorned sea holly.

LAPIDARY INSCRIPTION
WITH
EXPLANATORY NOTE

There was for him no more perfect epitaph
Than this from Shakespeare: "Nothing in his life
Became him like the leaving it." All those
Who knew him wished the son of a bitch in hell,
Despised his fawning sycophancy, smug
Self-satisfaction, posturing ways and pig-
Faced beady little eyes, his trite
Mind, and attested qualities of a shit,
And felt the world immeasurably improved
Right from the very moment that he left it.

———

Quintus, as what is called a man of the world,
You know how we keep the wheels of progress oiled
By what we call *prospicientia*,
Vorsichtichkeit, the prudent Boy Scout way
Of being prepared. For the obituary notice
When you shall slip behind the Great Portcullis,
I have prepared the modest sketch above
Conscientiously while you are still alive,
Omitting your worst features, as it behooves,
Not out of some *de mortuis* piety
But simply because they wouldn't be believed.

LONG-DISTANCE VISION

How small they seem, those men way in the distance.
Somehow they seem scarcely to move at all,
      And when they do, it is slowly,
Almost unwillingly. I bend my head
To my writing, look up half an hour later,
      And there they are, as if

Engaged in boring discussion, fixed in a world
Almost eventless, where it is somehow always
      Three in the afternoon,
The best part of the day already wasted,
And nothing to do till it's time for the first drink
      Of the uneventful evening.

I know, of course, binoculars would reveal
They are actually doing something—one doubles over
      (Is it with pain or laughter?),
Another hangs his jacket on the handle
Of his bicycle, tucks in his Versace sport-shirt
      And furtively checks his fly.

But the naked eyesight smooths and simplifies,
And they stand as if awaiting the command
      Of a photographer
Who, having lined them up in a formal group,
Will tell them to hold even stiller than they seem
      Till he's ready to dismiss them.

In much the same way, from a palace window,
The king might have viewed a tiny, soundless crowd
     On a far hill assembled,
Failing to see what a painter would have recorded:
The little domes, immaculate in their whiteness,
     At the foot of the cross.

SECRETS

The number of witches and sorceresses [has] everywhere become enormous. —JOHN JEWEL, BISHOP OF SALISBURY, 1559

When they fly through the air they turn invisible
But may sometimes be spotted by patient birding
   questers
At the witching hour in woods on the darkest possible
Moonless nights at the regular secret musters
Of their kindred spirits, these horrible Weird Sisters.

It is widely believed that lust is their ruling passion,
A legacy maybe of Puritan tradition,
Or because they are ugly, for they use some glutinous
   potion
To lure young farmhands into abject submission
Or orgies of loose sabbatical possession.

For their foul rites they render the fat of babies;
Spider and warted toad mix in their simples;
Heartless they are, and death is among their hobbies;
Nothing on earth is vile as their mildest foibles,
Cold as their tits, delicate as their thimbles.

POPPY

It builds like unseen fire deep in a mine,
      This igneous, molten wrath,
This smelting torture that rises with the decline
      Of reason, signifying death.

As when, fueled with suspicion, the coal-black
      Othello is wrought forge-hot,
Or when pouting Achilles lashes back
      At the whole Trojan lot

For the death of Patroclus: the one prepared to die
      In fury, to pit his life
Against a well-armed equal, the other to slay
      An innocent young wife;

Both, curiously, heroes. It is like that seething
      Pit, pitch-black, at whose lip
A petaled flame spreads crimsonly, bequeathing
      One or another sleep.

THE CEREMONY OF INNOCENCE

He was taken from his cell, stripped, blindfolded,
And marched to a noisy room that smelled of sweat.
Someone stamped on his toes; his scream was stopped
By a lemon violently pushed between his teeth
And sealed with friction tape behind his head.
His arms were tied, the blindfold was removed
So he could see his tormentors, and they could see
The so-much-longed-for terror in his eyes.
And one of them said, "The best part of it all
Is that you won't even be able to pray."
When they were done with him, two hours later,
They learned that they had murdered the wrong man.
And this made one of them thoughtful. Some years
    after,
He quietly severed connections with the others,
Moved to a different city, took holy orders,
And devoted himself to serving God and the poor,
While the intended victim continued to live
On a walled estate, sentried around the clock
By a youthful, cell phone—linked praetorian guard.

THE ROAD TO DAMASCUS

What happened? At first there were strange, confused
   accounts.
This man, said one, who had long for righteousness'
   sake
Delivered unto the death both men and women
In his zeal for the Lord, had tumbled from his mount,
Felled by an unheard Word and worded omen.
Another claimed his horse shied at a snake.

Yet a third, that he was convulsed by the onslaught
Of the falling sickness, whose victims we were urged
To spit upon as protection and in disgust.
Rigid in body now as in doctrine, caught
In a seizure known but to few, he lay in the dust,
Of all his fiercest resolves stunningly purged.

We are told by certain learned doctors that those
Thus stricken are granted an inkling of that state
Where *There Shall Be No More Time*, as it is said;
As though from a pail, spilled water were to repose
Midair in pebbles of clarity, all its weight
Turned light, in a glittering, loose, but stopped cascade.

The Damascene culprits now could rest untroubled,
Their delinquencies no longer the concern
Of this fallen, converted Pharisee. He rather
From sighted blindness to blind sight went hobbled
And was led forth to a house where he would turn
His wrath from one recusancy to another.

ELDERS

Ein dunkeler Schacht ist Liebe

As a boy he was awkward, pimpled, unpopular,
Disdained by girls, avoided by other boys,
An acned solitary. But bold and spectacular
The lubricious dreams that such a one enjoys.

He wandered apart, picked at his scabs, pinned down,
In the plush, delirious Minsky's of his mind,
High-breasted, long-thighed sirens who served his own
Terrible lusts, to which they became resigned,

And he thought himself masterful and accursed
As he pumped his flesh to climax, picturing wild
Virgins imploring him to do his worst,
And every morning he left his bedding soiled.

And so it went year by tormented year,
His yearnings snarled in some tight, muddled sensation
Of violence, a gout of imperiousness, fear
And resentment yeasting in ulcered incubation.

When he was old he encountered someone else
Enslaved by similar dreams and forbidden seethings,
Another dissatisfied, thrummed by the same pulse,
Who brought him where they both could observe
    bathing

In innocent calm voluptuous Susanna,
Delicate, and a quarter of his age,
Her flesh as white and wonderful as manna,
Exciting them both to desires engorged with rage.

SARABANDE ON ATTAINING THE AGE
OF SEVENTY-SEVEN

The harbingers are come. See, see their mark;
White is their colour, and behold my head.

Long gone the smoke-and-pepper childhood smell
Of the smoldering immolation of the year,
Leaf-strewn in scattered grandeur where it fell,
Golden and poxed with frost, tarnished and sere.

And I myself have whitened in the weathers
Of heaped-up Januarys as they bequeath
The annual rings and wrongs that wring my withers,
Sober my thoughts and undermine my teeth.

The dramatis personae of our lives
Dwindle and wizen; familiar boyhood shames,
The tribulations one somehow survives,
Rise smokily from propitiatory flames

Of our forgetfulness until we find
It becomes strangely easy to forgive
Even ourselves with this clouding of the mind,
This cinerous blur and smudge in which we live.

A turn, a glide, a quarter-turn and bow,
The stately dance advances; these are airs
Bone-deep and numbing as I should know by now,
Diminishing the cast, like musical chairs.

I.M.E.M.

To spare his brother from having to endure
Another agonizing bedside vigil
With sterile pads, syringes but no hope,
He settled all his accounts, distributed
Among a few friends his most valued books,
Weighed all in mind and heart and then performed
The final, generous, extraordinary act
Available to a solitary man,
Abandoning his translation of Boileau,
Dressing himself in a dark well-pressed suit,
Turning the lights out, lying on his bed,
Having requested neighbors to wake him early
When, as intended, they would find him dead.

"THE DARKNESS AND THE LIGHT
ARE BOTH ALIKE TO THEE"

PSALMS 139:12

Like trailing silks, the light
Hangs in the olive trees
As the pale wine of day
Drains to its very lees:
Huge presences of gray
Rise up, and then it's night.

Distantly lights go on.
Scattered like fallen sparks
Bedded in peat, they seem
Set in the plushest darks
Until a timid gleam
Of matins turns them wan,

Like the elderly and frail
Who've lasted through the night,
Cold brows and silent lips,
For whom the rising light
Entails their own eclipse,
Brightening as they fail.

NOTES

Flight Among the Tombs

"Death the Hypocrite": "Some bristlecone pines are the oldest living things on earth. . . . a total of seventeen bristlecone pines have been found which, still living and growing, are over 4,000 years old, the oldest some 4,600 years old." Andreas Feininger, *Trees*.

"Death the Poet": *Et nunc in pulvere dormio* (And now I sleep in the dust) is appropriated from a refrain in John Skelton's "Lament for the Death of the Noble Prince Edward the Fourth," which, in turn, was borrowed from an anonymous Middle English lyric that begins, "I hadde richesse, I hadde my helthe. . . ."

"Death the Punchinello": Some lines of Shakespeare's Richard of Gloucester (from *Henry VI*) have been appropriated, as has the last line, taken from Tristan Corbière's *"Le Crapaud."*

"Death the Copperplate Printer": Metaphors in the opening stanzas are borrowed from emblems, some of them identified by Rosemond Tuve in *A Reading of George Herbert*, where she writes of "the use of a set of conceits clustered around the ancient symbol of Christ as the miraculous grape-bunch," and remarks that this is "closely connected with various other symbols and conceits: Christ in the winepress of the Cross . . ." Jacob Cornelisz van Oostsanen's brown-ink drawing, *Allegory of the Sacrifice of the Mass* (*The Age of Bruegel*, National Gallery of Art) employs the same conceit in visual form. "Dutch Bath" is the name of a mordant used in copperplate etching; it is composed of dilute hydrochloric acid mixed with chlorate of potash. Saint Margaret Clitherow (1556–1586), a devout Roman Catholic convert from the Anglican Church, was pressed to death with an 800-pound weight for harboring Catholic clergy.

"Death the Scholar": Stagirite = Aristotle

"The Message": Adapted from a poem by Meleager in the Greek Anthology.

"The Mysteries of Caesar": Antinous was the favorite of the emperor Hadrian, by whose command statues of the young man, after his death, were set up in major cities throughout the empire.

"The Life of Crime": The poem was prompted by a passage in Mayhew's *London Labour and the London Poor.*

"Proust on Skates": Engelmann's Star is an elaborate pattern for figure skating, devised by one E. Engelmann, the Austrian skating champion of Europe in 1894. The "view of Delft" is a Vermeer painting that deeply impressed and affected Proust when he saw it in the Mauritshuis at The Hague in 1902.

"A Death in Winter": Sleep as "the death of each day's life," *Macbeth*, II, ii; "who's in, who's out," *King Lear*, V, ii; "trepidation of the spheres," John Donne, "A Valediction Forbidding Mourning"; Henry James referred to the Piazza San Marco as "a great drawing room, the drawing room of Europe"; statuary in the Luxembourg Gardens figures in Brodsky's poem-sequence "Twenty Sonnets to Mary Queen of Scots"; the hawk and snow are borrowed from Brodsky's poem "The Hawk's Cry in Autumn"; the "sensors" and "scanners" at the beginning owe something to the "instruments" in the opening of Auden's poem "In Memory of William Butler Yeats," just as "the sovereignty of the word" is indebted to Auden's homage to "language" in the same poem.

The Darkness and the Light

"Mirror": *A Mirror for Magistrates,* a sequence of poems by many hands concerning the theme of the Fall of Princes, of men of great authority and power, containing an *Induction,* and an account of the downfall of Henry, Duke of Buckingham, both by Thomas Sackville, Earl of Dorset.

"Samson": Judges 13:1–5

"Rara Avis in Terris": The poem was composed to accompany the anniversary gift of a brooch described in the final stanza.

"A Fall": *Pisse-Vache,* mentioned by Byron in an October 9, 1816, letter to John Murray as "one of the finest torrents in Switzerland."

"Haman": Esther 3:5–11

"A Certain Slant": The poem had its origin in a sentence in a story called "The Boys," by Anton Chekhov.

"Saul and David": I Samuel 16:14–23

"The Hanging Gardens of Tyburn": The poem is based on folklore concerning the mandrake plant, which was long believed to have magic properties. According to one botanical handbook, "its roots were an integral part of every witch's cauldron, its berries . . . used as an opiate and love potion. It was common knowledge in medieval times that the mandrake grew under the gallows from the dripping semen of hanged men. Pulled from the ground the root emitted wild shrieks and those who heard them were driven mad" (*Folklore and Symbolism of Flowers, Plants and Trees,* by Ernst and Johanna Lehner, p. 91).

"Judith": Judith 10:1–23

"Lot's Wife": Genesis 19:15–28

"Sacrifice": Genesis 22:1–19

"The Witch of Endor": I Samuel 28:3–25

"The Bequest": Vaillant, a.k.a. Pierre Chastellain (though by some these are held to be two entirely different persons) was a member of the circle of Charles d'Orléans.

"Miriam": Exodus 15:20 f; Numbers 12:1–15; Deuteronomy 24:9

"Secrets": One of the folk names for the foxglove is "witch's thimbles."

"The Road to Damascus": Acts 9. See also *From Jesus to Paul,* by Joseph Klausner, pp. 325–30.

"Elders": Daniel 13; Minsky's was a striptease/burlesque theater in the Times Square area of Broadway in the late 1930s.

A NOTE ON THE TYPE

The text of this book was set in Walbaum, a typeface designed by Justus Erich Walbaum in 1810. Walbaum was active as a typefounder in Goslar and Weimar from 1799 to 1836. Though the letter forms of this face are patterned closely on the "modern" cuts then being made by Giambattista Bodoni and the Didot family, they are of a far less rigid cut. Indeed, it is the slight but pleasing irregularities in the cut that give this typeface its humane quality and account for its wide appeal. In its very appearance Walbaum jumps boundaries, having a look more French than German.

Composed by Creative Graphics, Inc.,
Allentown, Pennsylvania

Printed and bound by R. R. Donnelley & Sons, Inc.,
Harrisonburg, Virginia

Designed by Soonyoung Kwon